Daniel Greenleaf Thompson

The Philosophy of Fiction in Literature

An Essay

Daniel Greenleaf Thompson

The Philosophy of Fiction in Literature
An Essay

ISBN/EAN: 9783337071738

Printed in Europe, USA, Canada, Australia, Japan

Cover: Foto ©ninafisch / pixelio.de

More available books at **www.hansebooks.com**

THE

PHILOSOPHY OF FICTION

IN LITERATURE

AN ESSAY

BY

DANIEL GREENLEAF THOMPSON

AUTHOR OF "A SYSTEM OF PSYCHOLOGY ;" "THE PROBLEM OF EVIL;"
"THE RELIGIOUS SENTIMENTS OF THE HUMAN MIND ;"
" SOCIAL PROGRESS," ETC., ETC.

NEW YORK AND LONDON
LONGMANS, GREEN, & CO.
1890

TO

CERTAIN GOOD FRIENDS OF MINE,

OF BOTH SEXES,

WHO ARE WRITERS

OF FICTION,

I RESPECTFULLY DEDICATE

THIS BIT OF PREACHING,

IN A DEPARTMENT IN WHICH THEY HAVE

SUCCESSFULLY PRACTISED.

New York, Sept. 1, 1890.

CONTENTS.

viii CONTENTS.

CHAPTER IX.

THE PHILOSOPHY OF FICTION
IN LITERATURE.

CHAPTER I.

THE OFFICE OF FICTION IN LITERATURE.

WHEN I have finished "Romola," by George
Eliot, the first and most obvious thing to be noted
upon reflection is that the book has interested
me sufficiently to cause me to read it through.
If, then, encouraged by this experience, and believing a novel to be a novel, I take up "Sir
Charles Grandison," I may find, after reading a
portion, that I grow tired, lay the book down, and
refuse to recur to it. I am bored, and the thought
of continuing is irksome. Clearly, then, all tales
are not interesting. Again, I am led to the perusal of M. Zola's "La Terre." My attention is
held ; I am presently shocked, then disgusted. I
throw the pamphlet into the fire and open the
windows to air the room. But my friend Jones
tells me he is very fond of "Sir Charles Grandi-

I

son."   He thinks novel writing has improved very
little since the days of Richardson, and he does
not like George Eliot.   My friend Smith read "La
Terre" through, and while, being a church-mem-
ber, he could not say he approved of the work, he
was interested, and thought there was something
virile about it, as there is in the dramas of Shakespeare.   At least he was sure the book would sell.

It is thus evident that whether a book is to us
readable or not depends on our respective mental constitutions, as does also the question of
approval or disapproval.   What is literary meat
to one man is poison to another.   If one person
likes devil-fish, to him devil-fish is good, although
there may not be many who have such an appetite.   To the Indiana drummer who excited
" Rev." Joseph Cook's wrath by eating raw steak,
bloody beef was a great delicacy.   He relished
and assimilated it.   Similarly, when we say a
book is good or bad, our judgment is formed by
our own likings, and our ideas of what is good for
other people as based upon our tastes.   But the
diversity in human nature is so great that such a
judgment, founded upon individual notions and
preferences, is a hazardous one to make.   We discover that a very intricate problem is presented
when we are called upon to value a literary work,
for we have, in the first place, to take into account
the immense variety of human wants ; and, if an
ethical element is introduced into our considera-

tions, the whole field of moral science, with its countless questions of casuistry, is opened.

Literature involves the preservation and communication of thought, using the latter term not in the sense of reasoned discourse, but in a broader application indicative of the whole of intellectual life with its emotional and volitional dependencies implied. Literature, therefore, may be a record of any part of human experience, so far as it is possible for words to express it; and this record, being also a means of communication, may induce a repetition of the experience or may furnish a stimulus to other experiences suggested by it. Hence literature affects conduct and is potent in both individual and social development.

Literature may be a record of what a person has perceived without, of what he has felt within, of what he has inferred and imagined, and of what he has done. The second and the last of these furnish autobiography. The third is indirect autobiography, indeed; but its characteristic is the expression of the mental life of the individual in constructed forms, which, though they are the product of experience, are not themselves given in any primary feeling or perception. His inferences are generalized from his primary experiences; his fictions of imagination are ideal creations. There remains the first class, which is purely historical, a chronicle of what is and has been in the world about us, embracing both natural and social history and covering all of the universe with which the individual mind has any communication.

Fiction, as the name imports, belongs to the third of the classes thus roughly marked out. It is a construction of human life and society which is not an exact reproduction of actual individuals, or of social life, nor of incidents of any particular series of events. The variation from historical accuracy may be slight, or may extend very far; but the narrative must furnish a sufficient departure to exclude it from the category of historical accounts. To be sure, many so-called histories are really novels, and many historical novels are more valuable as history than the professedly accurate chronicles; but the distinction is as stated: and in these latter cases the writer merely throws upon the reader who wishes to take the trouble the burden of disentangling the true and the fictitious, while those who do not care are content that the account may be either.

The form of fiction may be prose or verse, but usage has confined the term to such prose or verse as contains a movement of personality, a narrative of events—to the story, the tale, the novel. Hence, essays are not fiction, though Plato's " Dialogues " might not inappropriately be considered so, as they fulfil some of the most important conditions named. But in these productions the narrative is subordinate to the reasoning, and the reader's attention is never fixed upon the incident, unless it be in that account of the death of Socrates near the end of the "Phædo," and perhaps in one or two other places to a less degree. So that the " Dialogues " can scarcely even be reckoned as dramatic fiction. Nor can we include under the term descriptive poetry, like Goldsmith's " Deserted Village " ; nor reflective, like Bryant's " Thanatopsis "; nor didactic, like Wordsworth's "Excursion "—though all are works of the creative imagination. On the other hand, the great epics, like the " Iliad," the "Odyssey," " The Inferno," " Paradise Lost," are clearly poetical fiction, and more evidently still such narratives as Chaucer's " Canterbury Tales."

But restriction in the use of the word has gone so far that when one speaks of *Fiction* we understand prose fiction in the form of the story or novel. I shall make such usage the excuse for taking this form of literature as the principal topic of the present discussion, though most of what I shall have occasion to say will apply equally well to the tale in verse. Poetical composition, however, seems to demand a separate treatment, especially on the artistic side. The same thing is true of dramatic literature—the most intricate and difficult of all literary construction. It will hence be better if I leave these departments of fictitious literature without further treatment than may be involved in an occasional reference or illustration.

As was remarked at the outset, the first thing to be observed in reflecting upon the fact that we have read a novel is that it is interesting enough for us to have gone through it. Nevertheless, it is no doubt the case that many people have read novels in which they were not interested, impelled thereto by a stern feeling of duty created by the importunities of friends, or by the pride of a professional novel-reader who must keep up his reputation, or by general popular sentiment that a particular story is good. But there is no general moral obligation resting upon the community to read any production of this kind, as there is to read the Bible, or even the history of one's country. Common sentiment allows people to read or to avoid reading novels because they like or dislike them. This circumstance reveals the chief value of such works. They are primarily important in their artistic aspect. They are born of art, and as such their first office is to interest, to amuse, to please.

Yet it is quite certain that in order to please regard must be had to the sources of pleasure in the human mind. A story is artificial and does not of itself give pleasure naturally, as does a beautiful color, a musical sound, a cheering warmth when one is chilled. There must be some regard for artistic principles. An ungrammatical narrative, for instance, at once offends; as also does such a dialogue unless the irregular speech is made to emanate from a character in whom it would be natural. Similarly, vulgarities of expression given as the language of the author displease and disgust. Clumsiness, crudity, tediousness, tautology, commonplace, and many other offences against good taste have to be carefully avoided. There are all forms of beauty, symmetry, sublimity, grandeur, and their opposites, to be apprehended and felt in the reading of a book, and they have the most potent influence in fixing our estimate of it.

But it must be recollected that the sense of beauty is in no small degree dependent upon truth. No tale can be regarded as a work of fine art which does not have regard in its unfolding to a certain amount of congruity with the order of nature. By this it is not meant that entirely fanciful creations do not interest, for exactly the contrary is the case. " Gulliver's Travels," the " Munchausen" stories, and the vast number of popular fairy tales bear ample witness to this fact. Even absurdity is sometimes very delightful in all its degrees, from the mild ridiculousness of Mr. Frank R. Stockton's " Casting Away of Mrs. Lecks and Mrs. Aleshine," to the utter nonsense of the " Wogly Bird and Ginko Tree." But there must be a coherence and harmony in exhibiting the improbable or nonexistent. The plan or idea must be consistently maintained and developed. By preserving such a unity, the demands of the sense of truth are satisfied. The necessity for doing this with skill increases as mankind becomes more scientific. The ignorant mind is satisfied with the most extraordinary *bouleversements*, catastrophes, and productive effects wrought by gods and demons, and even by the *deus ex machina ;* because such things seem perfectly natural and probable when the belief in the existence of spiritual agencies, moving arbitrarily, is present. But the scientifically trained mind will have none of such trifling. A material or human cause must be adduced to account for everything, or the reader sneers and condemns. When the novel-writer gets out of the region of the purely fanciful and deals with the experiences of human beings in the world as it is, there is an absolute necessity that he conform to the natural conditions of his *locus in quo* and its inhabitants. Mr. Rider Haggard, in his tales of South African adventure, would have been laughed down if he had merely reproduced the incidents, the appearance of country, and the game that would be found in a hunting expedition in the north of England ; as uproariously as would an author describing a fox-hunt in the latter region who should allow his hunters suddenly to start an elephant. Walter Scott never would have succeeded with the " Waverley Novels " had he not made his descriptions consistent with their times ;

nor would the great artists who have portrayed
character, like Shakespeare, Molière, and Balzac,
have commanded the attention of the world, if
they had not presented to us men and women who
were typical of their times and circumstances, and
for whose existence in the story there was scientific warrant.

Again, the moral quality of a story, its scenes
and characters, is not and cannot be ignored. People who are animated by strong moral purposes
will be governed in their judgment of a novel by
its supposed ethical influences. To those who
believe that the breaking up of old theological
notions is a gain for morality, " Robert Elsmere "
is most admirable; while to those who esteem it
immoral to loosen the hold of ancient dogmas
and creeds, the story is thoroughly bad and most
reprehensible. No doubt the artistic merit or de-
merit of the book in question is, in the minds of
great numbers who read it, fixed and settled by its
moral character according to their views. We
may say all this is most unjust; but the fact remains, that mankind is so constituted that such
injustice is inevitable.

Without going further into detail, it is evident
that the office of fiction in literature is a very
complex one. It contributes to satisfy our crav-
ings for beauty, for truth, and for goodness; but
how to balance these properly is the serious problem. We must come back to our original propo-

sition; namely, that the prime requisite of a novel is that it shall interest. Our inquiry, then, must be: What are the things that interest? What does interest mean? And what are its bearings upon human life and happiness?

CHAPTER II.

INTEREST.

WHATEVER attracts and detains the attention interests, for this attraction and detention is what interest means. Any impact of sufficient force will secure attention for the moment. It may be arrested and held by a sensation which is pleasurable or painful; but if there be pain, an effort is made to get away from the object producing pain, and to expel the painful consciousness. This effort may not be successful, but it will be continued or repeated until the cause of pain is removed or unconsciousness supervenes. If the sensation be pleasurable, the attention is detained until the pleasurable quality fades out, or some new object is presented of greater sensational power. So far, then, as sensational experiences are concerned, the attention varies directly as the quantity of sensation.

But in the representative mental life the volitional law of the avoidance of pain, just alluded to, has a wider scope for its operation, because the higher the degree of mental development, the greater is the volitional control of the mind over its own states. Hence, that which is painful is more speedily dismissed, the mind refusing to dwell upon disagreeable or pain-producing suggestions. I cannot escape a harsh, disagreeable noise except by getting away from it, and until I do this I am forced to give it attention. But if I only remember that noise, the unpleasant associations of themselves tend to drive the recollection away and replace it by something else. Anything that suggests the disagreeable in our past experience we aim to put out of mind.

When we read a book, if the feelings aroused are unpleasant, it is quite within our power to throw it down and have no more of it. Unless we are bound hand and foot and forced to listen to the reading of some one else, we can control the situation. The question of interest then resolves itself into the broader one of what produces pleasurable and what produces painful emotion.

If, however, the statement be left thus, a distinction of immense importance will be overlooked. This distinction arises from the fact that what hurts my fellow-being does not necessarily pain me. On the contrary, it is true that I may derive much pleasure from my neighbor's woe. It does not deprive me of pleasurable interest in a work of fiction, therefore, to find that it depicts experiences painful to somebody, so long as they are not painful to me. My sympathetic likes and dislikes must be considered. In reading " Maiwa's

Revenge," by Mr. Rider Haggard, for instance, it gives the reader great satisfaction to have the old barbarian chief caught and horribly tortured in the "Thing-that-bites." If, on the other hand, the victim had been the captive Englishman who had been designed for such a fate, the feelings aroused would have been decidedly unpleasant, and we should have begun to find fault with the author. The visiting of punishment upon some one we deem worthy to receive it is grateful to our feelings, while the triumph of whatever we consider vicious and wicked is exceedingly offensive.

Hence, tragedy, woe, suffering in the most horrible forms, may impart a quality of interest to a novel if they are so introduced as to agree with the reader's sentiments. But this is not the whole of the matter. They may interest quite irrespective of our sympathies, where the predatory lusts are so strong in the human mind that murder and cruelty are relished for their own sake. There are many people so constituted, to whom scenes of carnage are agreeable. The most, indeed, would relish a realistic account of a bull-fight, not because they have any sympathy with either bull, but because they like a fight. The same thing is true of wars between human beings, though in the latter case there is generally something more than an interest in mere bloodshed.

We shall consider the bearings of this trait of

human nature upon our subject more fully in a subsequent chapter. It is mentioned now only to illustrate the point that interest in a story means the pleasurable interest which it excites in the reader through his own sympathies and antipathies. The extent of that interest among those who read depends upon the number of people who agree sufficiently in character to be similarly affected. What would have pleased the ten just men in Sodom, had there been that number, would not interest the remaining thousands ; while a story like " Mlle. Giraud, ma Femme," * or a " Marriage below Zero,"† which would no doubt delight the multitudes of that city, would be abhorrent to the ten.

For the purposes of this essay, the sources of pleasure and pain may be grouped as æsthetic, scientific, and moral, according to the lines marked out in the preceding chapter. The true theory of pleasure and pain is, in my judgment, that which connects the two with the conservation of life. Pleasures have relation to three general functions: (1) growth ; (2) preservation of the integrity of the mind and body; (3) reproduction. Correspondingly, pains have relation to: (1) retardation ; (2) disintegration ; (3) annihilation. Using the most general terms, the pleasures of the mind are: (1) to acquire ; (2) to possess and conserve ; and (3)

---

* Belot.   † Alan Dale.

to perpetuate.* Thus the fundamental and basic pleasures of human life are appetitive, and all others are differentiations from and refinements of these. But the interests now under consideration are wholly representative. They are not primary, like the pleasure of repletion after a good meal. They affect human happiness indirectly, not directly. Novels are not necessities of life, nor are they immediately deleterious or destructive.

When we take note of the distinguishing characters of æsthetic pleasures we shall readily perceive the true location of those enjoyments we derive from works of fiction. Æsthetic pleasures arise in connection with objects which are not present for the purpose of ministering to our necessities, or at least so far as that idea is not suggested. Secondly, they arise in connection with objects which are without disagreeable accompaniments, or so far forth as such objects are without them. Thirdly, they spring up with objects whose enjoyments are not restricted to a single mind, or which do not perish with the using. A novel obviously satisfies the first and the third of these conditions. It is a constructive product to be enjoyed by many minds and not to perish with the using. Whatever else it is, it has at least this æsthetic basis. Its further and complete æsthetic character is derived from its conformity to the

---

* "System of Psychology," by the present author, Part VIII., ch. lx.

second condition, and its success depends upon the preponderance of the agreeable over the disagreeable.

Here intervene the other offices of fiction which we remarked in the last chapter. We can impart information and can influence conduct by a story. Hence the scientific and the moral quality of fiction. The relations of these three elements to each other we shall consider later. But it may safely be said that, however much scientific and moral characteristics in a novel may influence us, we never can divest the work of its fundamentally æsthetic character ; and we shall have seriously to ask whether we do not lose much more than we gain when we attempt to subordinate that which is in itself æsthetic to any sort of didactic purposes.

CHAPTER III.

THE SCIENTIFIC VALUE OF FICTION.

WHEN the fond parent wishes to impress some truth upon the mind of his child so strongly as to make certain that it will not be eradicated, he is very apt to include it in a story. The familiar " Once-upon-a-time " will detain the youngster's attention and make him a ready listener, when if the fact, to impart the knowledge of which is the object of the tale, were stated baldly, the child would not receive it; or, if he did, would not long remember. Without the narrative there is no interest; the mind fails to take hold of and incorporate with itself the things presented.

A great deal of valuable information has, no doubt, been imparted to youth in this way. Tales of hunting and fishing adventure, like Capt. Mayne Reid's series, of which "The Boy Hunters" and "The Young Voyageurs" are samples, have both delighted and instructed many. So, likewise, much mechanical and other applied science has been inculcated by works like the "Rollo"* books.

---

* Abbott.

Again, Col. Thomas W. Knox, in his "Boy Trav-
eller" volumes, has been highly successful, setting
forth in a fictitious narrative much interesting and
valuable knowledge respecting remote lands of the
earth and their denizens. The object of such productions is primarily educational. They aim to
instruct through fiction, employed as a device to
hold the attention and arouse interest.

This, of course, is not pure fiction in the sense
in which we are considering fiction as a theme;
but story-telling of this sort illustrates most
plainly the use to which fiction may be put in
imparting knowledge. And it is by no means
unusual to find in works wherein the fictitious
narrative is the chief distinctive characteristic,
scientific information, upon which many readers
will lay the most stress; and for which especially,
or even solely, will they esteem the production.
Not to speak further of natural history, though
there is not a little to be learned in this department from many good novels, it is evident that
geography, physical and political, is taught very
extensively and effectively by tales which will not
be denied a place with fiction proper. If we class
descriptions of natural scenery and of towns in
this category, we shall at once meet with one of
the most charming features of story-composition
in all literatures. Such descriptions, indeed, perhaps generally derive their greatest value from the
æsthetic elements, from the manner and style of

diction rather than from the knowledge imparted; but there is still a good deal of interest awakened by the fact that the reader is learning something. It is often because something may be acquired from them, supposably true, that Walter Scott's works are highly commended. Many a person has obtained his ideas of the appearance of certain localities entirely from some tale he has read. Even in a writer who can by no means be classed as a typically descriptive author (I use the term as applied to natural scenery) we often come upon pages of most excellent description, as the reader of " Wanda " * will doubtless call to mind. Again, the vivid pictures of shore and sea presented in William Black's novels have possessed the minds of many more completely than the movement of life in the development of the plot.

Still more true is this line of remark when the department of history is included. The historical novel has been at times the leading type of fiction. This resulted at one period from the eminence of Scott, in England, and of Cooper, in America. More recently, Louisa Mühlbach, whose history is unhistorical, and Georg Ebers, who strives to be as accurate as if writing scientific treatises, may be cited as story-writers of this class. The best of these authors have aimed to make their historical statements reliable. The critical and reading

---

* Ouida.

public, recognizing that the purpose of the story is partly to teach history, has insisted that what is stated as fact shall be fact, and have estimated the authors accordingly.

From the scientific point of view we have, then, the geographical, the botanical, the zoölogical, and the historical novel. We might add the astronomical, if we take into account the Jules Vernes who have written voyages to the moon and dealt with life in the planets. The publication of the " Strange Manuscript found in a Copper Cylinder "* would justify another class, that of the geological novel. Taking all together, natural history, in its various branches, and the history of human life will comprise the scientific elements in fictitious literature.

The last-named category, however, includes much more than has been indicated. Its suggestion leads us to a genuine scientific value of the novel, which is often overlooked. A purely fictitious representation of human life and society, which is recognized as a type of actually existing conditions, is of scientific importance, not only because it is true, but because the truth cannot be set forth in any other way. We cannot take a definitely known individual, dissect his character and exhibit his unworthy traits, without incurring the risk of a libel suit ; or, if we make him too

---

* De Mille.

angelic, without exciting all sorts of ridicule from
those who do not agree with our estimate. More
than one writer has suffered seriously from even
the suspicion of having intended some living person in the portrayal of a fictitious character. It
may be remembered that the author of a story
called "Cape Cod Folks" aroused great excitement and indignation, not many years ago, because
it was believed she had maliciously "done up" a
whole community. Nor is it always safe to tell
the truth about the dead. It is very hard to get
just historical accounts of popular idols. The first
edition of Sparks's "American Biography" contained mention of a certain *liaison* of George Wash-
ington ; but so much disfavor was manifested on
this account that it was taken out of subsequent
editions. It would have been very dangerous to
the author to have published even ten years ago
that circumstantial account of Abraham Lincoln's
unhappy domestic life which Mr. Herndon's book
has just presented.* The diary of the Emperor
Frederick III. of Germany is sealed up, and no
one can get at it, much less use it for historical
purposes. Not only is it impossible oftentimes to
print correct biographies, but any direct criticism
of governmental, religious, and social institutions
is utterly forbidden at many times and in many
places. The only way in which people can be

---

* 1889.

fully instructed, then, as to social conditions is by fiction. The works of M. Zola and the Russian realists are examples of this kind of education. The only method of obtaining any thorough knowledge, at least of contemporary character and society, its formative influences, the ultimate results of particular courses of action, existing tendencies toward weal or woe, is through the analysis and depiction of the novelist. The novel, then, has a very decided and marked psychological, ethological, and sociological utility.

CHAPTER IV.

THE MORAL VALUE OF FICTION.

ALMOST everybody assumes that a book must have a purpose, and people are incorrigible in their habit of inquiring what its effect is likely to be. They mean, its moral effect. If they consider this to be bad, they very unwarrantably jump to the conclusion that it proceeded from an evil purpose. Then both the book and the author are condemned.

If an author's object apparently be to interest or amuse, with no ulterior moral aim, the mass of readers generally put his work on a lower plane. If a didactic character is evident, the book is much better. Many persons are always looking for a " *Hæc fabula docet*," and are much disappointed if they fail to find it. I fancy this peculiarity arises simply from the fact that a book was primarily, and is now among those who read little regarded solely, as an instrument of education. Books are given children to teach them something—reading itself, spelling, computation, geography. When a story appears the first questions asked are, "What is it for?" "What does it teach?" "What good does it do?" It is easy to answer these questions if applied to the zoölogical novel. Neither is the historical tale troublesome. It is a good thing to know something about animals, and the history of human events is not to be despised.

It takes a cultivated mind to enjoy flowers for their own sake. A farmer may be interested in apple-blossoms, but it is not for their beauty that he looks at them. It is solely as an indication of the coming yield of fruit. If he should meet with a strange plant in the woods, his attention attracted by a highly colored flower, his first thought would be, "What is it good for?" If it be of no use, or in any wise deleterious, it is cut down ruthlessly as a noxious weed. Precisely so does the average mind, and, I am sorry to say, sometimes the cultivated mind, deal with literature. If it does not directly teach something useful or good, it is rejected.

Now, a novel may have a moral effect in many ways. It may influence positively to good conduct and away from evil. It also may have negative effects in the same direction, or the opposite. There may be interjected here and there moral precepts and reflections, with arguments to prove how much better it is to worship Jehovah than Baal. Stories are frequently told in this style and win great popularity. No doubt, so far as they influence at all, they are morally beneficial. They

are not very nourishing, however. Direct preaching in a "moral tale" is not as readily absorbed
as natural history details are in the zoölogical
novel. It is much more tiresome. But if a moral
or religious tale could be constructed after the
Salvation Army manner of doing things—with
much that is startling and sensational—I am not
at all sure that the interlarded sermons would not
have more effect.

But this method of improving character and
conduct is very crude and is the least effectual.
A much greater influence can be exercised by the
development of plot in such a way as to indicate
the true relations of cause and effect in human life,
showing the results of good and evil conduct respectively. With regard to this, moral sentiment
has generally demanded a triumph of the good
in the event. Successful villany, in a narrative,
makes the reader uncomfortable at least ; and in
youthful or unbalanced minds may inspire to a
criminal course of life, through false apprehensions
of what such a life will bring. Thrilling stories of
crime have often induced to the commission of
crime. Boys every now and then run away from
home to fight Indians, after reading "dime
novels." Occasionally they try highway robbery
or burglary under similar inspiration. Therefore,
when a story exalts the criminal as a hero, and
makes his escape from justice matter for congrat-
ulation, the effect upon dispositions and conduct

is no doubt immoral. To what extent this immoral force is derived from the essential untruth
of such tales is a very serious question, to which
we shall refer in another chapter. At all events,
they are not read by the experienced and educated, and their influence over the most of those
who would read them is doubtless bad.

It would be going very far, though, to condemn
all novels which do not finally make their virtuous
characters happy and duly punish all their bad
people. When we come to consider the æsthetic
value of fiction and to make comparisons we shall
find there is intrinsic morality in a work of art.
But it is undeniable that the demand for a moral
purpose in a novel is so extensive that the question of moral influence must be regarded seriously.
Making heroes of murderers and pirates, and allowing them a reasonably happy and successful
life is certainly not wholesome from the moralist's
standpoint. A similar condemnation is apt to fall
upon the novelist who permits a good principle to
be vanquished in argument by a bad one. Sophis-
tries, evil insinuations, lies of all sorts can be made
to proceed from the mouth of characters in a
story and stand without effective opposition or
contradiction. No doubt harm may be done in
this way. False ideas may be inculcated and
youth corrupted. But we should be careful to
remember that there are differences of opinion as
to what is truth and what is truly moral. If a

Russian liberal were to write a romance in which persons appear who give utterance to revolutionary sentiments, the book would be considered by the government to be pernicious and would be suppressed. One living in a free country, however, would see nothing bad in it, and would rather applaud the sentiments. It must not be forgotten that one great value of fiction is that it may be made the vehicle of the free expression of opinions. Our disapproval of books as immoral should therefore be given cautiously. We must first be sure what is moral and what is immoral.

This whole subject of moral value in works of fiction, being educational, relates principally to undeveloped minds—ignorant or easily influenced adults, or the young of both sexes. The solicitude of parents for the welfare of their children makes them extremely jealous of any hurtful influences. A grown person of average intellectual strength is not so likely to be moved toward evil courses by reading a romance as he is by a conversation with a plausible but wicked acquaintance. There is an element of personal magnetism in the latter case which is wanting in the former. The influence of the book is not a persisting one ; though there may be conviction flowing from it, there is little persuasion. It may well be doubted if fully matured persons are often seduced into harmful courses, or materially modified in character by a novel. But it is quite true, on the other hand, that thought has been stimulated and important popular movements inaugurated and forwarded by works of fiction. "Uncle Tom's Cabin" is a very conspicuous illustration. A work that makes an impression in this way should never be condemned as immoral, whatever lesson it may inculcate. It is an expression of the thought in the minds of multitudes and symptomatic of an evolutionary movement that cannot be suppressed and will issue in some change necessitated by present conditions. Agitation and discussion is precisely what is most needed. And while we may totally disagree with the ideas of the author, the morality of liberty of expression is supereminent in such a case.

We shall not do more in this chapter than to point out very generally the sources of moral qualities in a work of fiction. It is sufficiently clear, I trust, that they are the possible and patent educational influences. This, of course, merely introduces the topic; which will continually recur, and, indeed, be forced upon us as we proceed. But it is better that we now turn to look upon the artistic side of the general subject.

CHAPTER V.

IN Chapter II. we found the work of fiction to be a product of the constructive powers of the human intellect; such product being an object not administering directly to our appetitive necessities nor satisfying them; an object susceptible of universal enjoyment, not perishing with the using; an object in which the disagreeable is minimized. The constructive power is the innate activity of the mind, now appearing as a reaction to environing forces, now as the initiatory power which operates upon the external world, the understanding which, as the German philosophers say, " makes nature."

Mental activity is a source of pleasure in itself, as is exemplified in the play-impulse. Mere exercise of intellectual powers is a joy, because that exercise tends toward growth and preservation. Inaction, save as a restful alternative, is disintegrating and destructive. Play, or the exercise of activity spontaneously without regard to further utility than lies in the exercise itself, is characteristically æsthetic. When an end is proposed, the movement toward that end is work, but in the achievement there arise emotions which are again of an æsthetic nature. Doing something, producing, accomplishing, causing, making experience, making nature—all involve that creative activity which lies at the foundation of art. There is truth in what M. Lucien Arréat says:[*] *" L'élément esthétique du travail ce n'est pas l'idée d'un effet utile, mais celle de la difficulté vaincue, et qui semble vaincue gratuitement."* [†]

It is undoubtedly the case, therefore, that any object fabricated by the hand of man which gives the impression of skill, of difficulties overcome, of a triumph of mind over matter, of successful contrivance, so far forth produces an æsthetic effect upon the spectator. This often contributes to heighten the admiration which comes from thoughts of the utility of the object. Frequently to the artistic mind it is the principal element in whatever pleasure is experienced. But, after all, we have indicated here only rudimentary and undifferentiated art. We are directed, however, to the subjective and creative character of artistic products. The idea of skill, of accomplishment, is always present in the fine as well as the mechanic arts.

---

[*] " La Morale dans le Drame l'Épopée et le Roman," ch. vi.

[†] " The æsthetic element in work is not the idea of a useful effect, but that of difficulty conquered, and which seems conquered freely."

The constructive activity is synthetic, as indeed is all mental activity. It unites a manifold of particulars into a whole, whose parts have an organic connection. It aims primarily to make this whole distinct and well defined. Although it uses the particular parts as material, it associates them into a unity clearly separate from other unities. This does not require that the parts shall be distinctly apprehended in detail. They must, however, be consonant with and contribute to the general unity. They are subordinate to the whole, which is the ideal construction. Hence a work of art must be an evident unity, capable of making an impression as such upon the one who is to enjoy it. Whether or not it have a "purpose," it must, at least, have a plan. It must have an idea, to which the details of working out are relevant and homogeneous. The general effect on the beholder must be centripetal, not centrifugal. The attention must be concentrated, not scattered.

The voluntary action of the mind is always selective. It chooses some things and rejects others. Its movement, already remarked, is toward pleasure and away from pain. Nevertheless, it cannot wholly escape the latter. Painful experiences force themselves upon us. The ends, then, which we propose to ourselves are ends of happiness, misery being eliminated. Thus we form ideals of existence, which are of better states and conditions than we actually encounter, and which we are all the time endeavoring to realize. So in art it is not enough merely to construct a unity of harmoniously related parts, but this integer must be so selected as to arouse agreeable feelings. It must satisfy our ideals of excellence. The sight of a beautiful landscape inspires pleasure of an æsthetic character. The reproduction of this landscape upon canvas or paper by the hand of the artist also gives delight, because it is a representation of a pleasurable experience. The same landscape, however, may be painted so as to fail utterly in repeating the agreeable impression. This may arise from inaccuracy in depicting the various objects. It also may occur because the artist fails to select those objects in the view which are most essential in creating the impression. If he introduces these last with correctness, he may be inaccurate in minor features and may even omit a great many things altogether. If he gets the right perspective, the true proportions of objects, the proper lights and shades, the general effects of color, he is successful. It is indispensable that he understand how to seize upon the chief factors of the total impression and reproduce them with fidelity in the picture.

Again, an æsthetic pleasure may be secured if the artist changes the landscape by varying its essential features, leaving out some and introducing others not in the scene originally. If this be done in obedience to an ideal of improvement, so long as those congruities are preserved which are essential to the conception of a landscape, the result is truly æsthetic and may be more pleasing than in the former case. The effect would be greatly marred, indeed, if the picture purported to present a view of some particular locality with which the beholder is familiar and he should see that it was untrue. But if it were so named as to indicate no special location, its artistic character would not be impaired by the departure from reality of which I have spoken.

Once more, an entirely imaginative landscape may be painted which will elicit admiration and seem more wonderful than any copy from nature, provided always that there are maintained faithfully "*les rapports et les dépendances mutuelles des parties.*" * The idea of a landscape must be realized and no violence done to it. Idealizing and improvement there may be, but not carried so far as to destroy the distinctive character of the picture.

We are now prepared for the remark that there may be an æsthetic value in a copy of nature, because nature is continually developing æsthetic emotions in the human mind. But not all nature does this. Much that we encounter in the physical world arouses feelings the very reverse of æsthetic.

---

* " The harmony and organic connection of the parts."—*Véron.*

The mere copying of a natural object does not result in a work of fine art. It may have that artistic merit of which we spoke a little while ago, which springs merely from the fact that it is a work of skill, a use of matter by mind, a combining of earth and oil to express an idea. But this consideration may be wholly offset by the repellent character of the object itself, respecting which there can be no interest in reproducing. More is required. It is æsthetic nature which must be reproduced to be of the most complete and the highest artistic value. The natural, if it be nonæsthetic, must be excluded, regarding the matter from the purely æsthetic point of view.

It is thus evident that we may justifiably divide works of art into two grand divisions, the one of reproductive and the other of creative art. As has been seen, the two may be mingled in the same product ; but the distinction will be found a useful one and important to be held in mind in judging artistic work.

Applying the foregoing observations to the form of literary construction which is the subject of this essay, we discover that we have both the reproductive and the creative varieties in varying proportions. At first thought we might say that the zoölogical and the historical novel furnish the best examples of the former. But, in fact, to the extent that they are zoölogical and historical, they are not fiction at all. They are supposably science, and though science may be presented artistically and have an æsthetic value, it is not there that we look for pure art. But whether history, natural or political, be written in an artistic manner, it is not our theme at present. Where, then, do we find reproductive art in fiction ?

We shall find it in description of scenery, of inanimate and animate objects, of the multifold products of man's activity which conform to the things seen in actual experience. These various objects may or may not be really existent. Frequently they are, but are transplanted from one locality to another with perhaps very different surroundings. Or, the scene may be laid in a well-known place and accurate descriptions given of what may actually be found there. This is the most common method of providing a setting for the human characters, of establishing a habitat for the movement of life. Where this is done, precisely the same principle applies as in the case of the landscape painter. The description must be of such a quality as to produce an æsthetic effect. The essential features must be seized upon and brought to the mind of the reader.

Reproductive art is also manifested in the characters and their action. However much the author may strive, he cannot get out of the circle of human experience. Men must be men, and women must be women. They must have passions, opinions, motives, instincts, appetites.

Knowing this, very many writers think the safe
way is to study some individual, who becomes the
prototype of the character in fiction. The shrewd
Yankee, the fickle Frenchman, the rampant and
obstreperous Irishman, the phlegmatic German,
the comical Negro, who are familiar in works of
fiction, have frequently their originals in real life.
All the physical and moral traits of humanity are
continually reproduced in current stories, the success of which is due in many instances to the accuracy of reproduction. This representation is,
of course, extended to the general aspects of social life in the way mentioned in the last part of
Chapter III. The historical novelists have done
this very extensively, but not more, after all, than
the schools of analytical writers. Dickens, Thackeray, Bulwer, George Eliot, Balzac, Mr. Howells,
Dr. Edward Eggleston—all present distinct, evident, and powerful reproductions of real life and
society. They reflect the times and the courses
of events of the places and periods of which they
write.

But just at this point we ought to note the entrance of creative art. Even if a character have a
living prototype, it is easy to modify it according
to the author's fancy. The plan of his work may
require the development of such thought and
action that a living person may be taken as a
basis, and traits he has not may be added unto
him. Then, again, some curious, well-emphasized

trait may be subtracted, like the rib from Adam's side, and a wholly ideal being may be constructed around it. Probably the most of novelists' characters are made up in this way or are composite productions, a head being obtained from one model, a heart from a second, a virtue from this, a weakness from the other, and so on. It is hard to separate the representation from the creation.

Another form of mixed reproduction and imagination occurs where the writer portrays an historical personage with some foundation of fact, supplemented by the writer's general conception, the truth of which is not, perhaps cannot be, ascertained. The hero is endowed with such qualities as the author thinks a man of his deeds ought to have had, and is made to act as such a personage would most probably have acted. In Miss Mühlbach's novels, before referred to, there is much of this sort of writing. Historical novels generally abound in such portraiture. Mr. Rider Haggard exemplifies it in " Cleopatra," both with respect to the Egyptian queen and to Antony. George Eliot has developed her Savonarola in " Romola" after this fashion. In all such instances only study will enable the reader to know what is historical and what is imaginative. Sometimes investigation will reveal fidelity, and at others gross libels will be found to have been perpetrated.

Beyond productions like these, creative art goes

on to limitless constructions of ideal characters, in which one sentiment or another dominates, and in which all possible evolutions and involutions of human feeling, thought, and volition are traced to their ultimate consequences, as imagined. The world of fiction is peopled with unique, grand, dwarfed, virtuous, wicked, beautiful, ugly individualities, which impress themselves in one way or another upon the readers of books, always exciting interest and receiving now admiration, and now detestation, according to the sentiments of those who make their acquaintance.

In depicting the action and reaction of social forces there is the same scale of variation, from simple reproduction to the most lofty ideal conceptions of what ought to be. Heaven has been imagined, and heavens on earth. The ideals of beauty intrinsic, of the beauty there is in truth and in goodness, have been used to produce and place before others, as universal property to be enjoyed forever, enough works of marvellous creation to stand, not only as monuments of what heights man's genius has already reached, but also to declare unto us convincingly the limitless capacities of the human mind.

We have hitherto been inquiring what objects arouse æsthetic feelings, but this does not wholly fulfil the requirements of the theme. We shall be unable to understand thoroughly the æsthetic value of fiction without a deeper study of the nature and meaning of æsthetic emotions in general. If works of art are those which arouse such emotions, what are the emotions themselves and their value? We shall, perhaps, be able to answer these questions sufficiently without wearying the reader too much with psychological detail ; but, in order to find any answer, a reference to the laws which express the constitution of the human mind is necessitated.

Pleasure satisfies. It suspends action except in furtherance of its continuance. It is an end in itself. It is a concomitant of vitality, an expression of the fulness of life. The more complete and unalloyed it is, the stronger is the sense of vital power, of permanence, of exhaustless energy. But change is necessary to life and to pleasure. Monotony of pleasure is a pain which moves to new exertion to attain something else. Life, then, is a struggle between life-giving and life-maintaining forces on the one hand, and disintegrating and destroying forces on the other. But pleasure is not wholly correspondent with physical life ; that is to say, the deterioration of the body and the failure of its appetites does not take away the capacity for pleasurable experience. This is owing to the representative power which in one of its exercises reproduces, though in less degree of intensity, pleasures previously enjoyed ; and in another out of the elements of past experiences produces new objects which excite pleasure. "*Le*

*plaisir est la jouissance actuelle des sens ; c'est une
satisfaction entière qui on leur accorde dans tout ce
qu'ils appètent ; et lorsque les sens epuisés veulent du
répos ou pour reprendre haleine ou pour se refaire,
le plaisir devient de l'imagination ; elle se plaît à
réfléchir au plaisir que sa tranquillité lui procure.*"*
It is quite true, therefore, that pleasures of imagination, both reproductive and productive, may
subsist in the midst of racking pain and with the
knowledge that life is ebbing.   But when they
are felt under such circumstances, it is still the case
that they are identical in their nature with pleasures experienced in exuberant health.   There
comes into the consciousness the same feeling of
satisfaction, of rest, of life, though it may not be
complete or long-continued.   For the moment,
however, the mind is lost in a conscious state
which is good in itself, though it almost instantly
be recalled to painful conditions. In the experience
of pleasure the person is taken out of time and
motion and change, into eternity, permanence, rest.
He simply is ; past and future are irrelevant. But
pain, even if it be merely uneasiness, reveals the
need of action and stimulates him to effort to real-

---

* "Pleasure is the actual experience of the senses. It is a complete satisfaction accorded to them in all that they seek ; and when
the senses, wearied, need repose, either to take breath or to acquire new strength, pleasure becomes an affair of the imagination.
This faculty takes delight in reflecting on the pleasure its own tran-
quillity procures for it."—"Memoires de Jacques Casanova de
Seingalt."

ize happiness under the guidance of his recollec-
tions of what has been and his ideals of what may
be.

Pleasure is thus always the same thing. It is
an ultimate consciousness which can only be understood by experience. It is the sense of life,
of existence, and the powers which existence implies. It varies only in respect to quantity. A
pleasure as pleasure is only greater or less than
another. The different kinds of pleasures receive
their distinctive character wholly from intellectual
attachments. We describe and define our pleasures and pains according to our intellectual ap-
prehension of the objects which are before the
mind when the pleasure is present, and which
may be regarded as its causes.* Therefore, having indicated what pleasurable feeling is in itself,
when we say that æsthetic pleasure is pleasure
aroused by those objects which we have defined
as æsthetic, we have compassed the whole matter,
so far as general explanation is possible. But in
order to a clearer understanding, there are some
things yet to be noted.

Æsthetic objects are chiefly apprehended by
the eye and the ear. A more close analysis would
show, I am persuaded, that these are not the
only æsthetic senses; but for the purposes of
this treatise we can rest content with taking into

---

* "System of Psychology," chaps. lix., xliii., xlv., lii.

account only objects of sight and hearing, inasmuch as they furnish substantially all the material for æsthetic perception as it is commonly understood. These, however, are distinctively and prominently representative senses, their objects deriving importance chiefly from and producing their effects mainly by means of the associations which they evoke in the mind. This is peculiarly the case with objects of sight in general and with spoken language. We need not here treat of the primary stimulation of light and sound, which is sensational in its nature. It is through perceptive activity, forming distinct and definite objects of their material and connecting these with past experiences, that the eye and the ear attain their transcendent importance as ministers to mental life.

It should be observed, further, that pleasures from æsthetic objects are contemplative. The one who enjoys them is not striving. He is a recipient, his mind only and not his body being active. He looks upon a beautiful picture or statue. He quiescently reads a book or listens to music. These stir within him thoughts and feelings of past delights and awaken ideals of new ones with inspirations to their realization. But it must not be thought that contemplation means intellectual inactivity. On the contrary, the representative or imaginative activities are stimulated, the increase of energy coming with the pleasurable contemplation expending itself in further reminiscence, in constructions, and in volitional impulses. And this leads us back to our observations at the commencement of the chapter, to the effect that the joy of activity for its own sake is æsthetic. Play is the symbol of exuberance of life and indicates strength and happiness, overflowing and demanding expenditure. The same fulness of vitality urges the artist to reproducing and creating, and, in our contemplation of his work, enters into our own pleasure and excites that admiration of skill of which we also spoke.

If we have correctly apprehended the nature of æsthetic pleasure, it will be seen that the appreciation of art and the art-impulse are inherent in the nature of man as a conscious being, and are not the products of civilization. They exist in the savage as well as in the enlightened, though exhibited in a different way. If only there be a representative faculty, there must be art and objects which excite æsthetic interest; and without a representative power, consciousness is not possible. That these statements are historically true will be seen by any one who familiarizes himself with the habits of primitive and barbarous men. He will find language, and with it oratory and poetry, music, the dance, always religion and also architecture; all of which distinctly declare the æsthetic sentiment. But as civilization advances, the objects which develop æsthetic interests change, those which were potent in a lower stage being of no influence or value whatever in the higher. Even in the same grade of enlightenment what will appeal to one will not appeal to another. This brings to view again the importance of variations of individual temperament and character in considering questions of the appreciation of works of art, to which we alluded at the beginning of the first chapter.

To return now to our special theme—works of fiction excite interest through language, and, prominently, written language. Language appeals both to the ear and the eye, but is primarily a means of communication between human beings addressed to the ear. If we bear this in mind, we shall more readily arrive at the exact value of fiction. We shall recur to the relations it bears to literature in general (Chapter I.). We shall perceive that the story or tale is something which one person (the author) has to tell others about real or possible relations of human beings to each other— about man in his individual development and in society. It is generically a means of communication between man and man. This is by no means all, but it is at least this. But in order to be æsthetic, it must be such a production as to interest and please the reader. As already remarked, it may accomplish this end either by reproduction or creation. The question, then, is suggested: How far should the writer of fiction cultivate reproductive and how far creative art? Is the truest art found in the one or the other? If we say in the latter, then how far is the former necessary for creation, since creation is only a new combination of the materials given us in nature? These questions will introduce an important controversy and will enable us to study a movement in literature which has recently become quite predominant.

CHAPTER VI.

REALISM AND IDEALISM.

IN considering the special topic of this chapter, it will be advantageous for us to reflect upon the thought contained in the two following quotations. The first is from a " History of English Prose Fiction," by Bayard Tuckerman : " A novelist, then, is realistic or not realistic according to the views which he and his readers entertain of nature. To the optimist, to the youthful and romantic, 'The Heart of Midlothian' and 'Guy Mannering' will seem a truthful representation of life. The more worldly and practical will find their idea of reality in 'The Mill on the Floss,' in 'Vanity Fair,' in the 'Prime Minister.' And finally, those whose tastes or lot has kept them 'raking in the dirt of mankind' will think their view of truth best expressed by 'Nana' and 'L'Assommoir.' "

The second passage is from the preface of " Pierre et Jean," by M. Guy de Maupassant : " Our eyes, our ears, our sense of smell, our sense of taste, differing as they do, create as many truths as there are men upon earth. And our minds, which receive the instruction of these organs, differently impressed, understand, analyze, and judge as if each of us belonged to a distinct race. Each one of us, therefore, forms for himself an illusion of the world, an illusion poetical, sentimental, joyous, melancholy, unclean, or dismal, according to his nature."

It seems, therefore, that whether a work conforms to nature or not depends in the reader's mind upon what he knows of nature; upon nature as it is to him. If a story is true to life, it means, to the ordinary reader at least, that life with which he is acquainted. It must appeal to his own experience.

Nevertheless, uninteresting subjects are often by some sort of artistic power made interesting; the common, the unlovely arrest our attention because of the excellence of the reproduction. In his little treatise for beginners, entitled "The Elements of Drawing," Mr. Ruskin says: "Go into your garden or into the road and pick up the first round or oval stone you can find, not very white, nor very dark; . . . now, if you can draw that stone you can draw anything; I mean, anything that is drawable. Many things (sea-foam, for instance) cannot be drawn at all, only the idea of them more or less suggested; but if you can draw the stone rightly, everything within reach of art is also within yours." So it is with the portrayal of character. Select any person

whom you know and will take as a model for your
description. No matter how common the person
may be, if you can reproduce him to the mind by
words, so that he stands forth a distinct, living
personal character, you have mastered the prime
essential of the art of fiction. Without the power
to do this you cannot succeed at all. If you have
that power, you may not, indeed, become a great
novelist, but you can write a novel.

Let us see what this portraiture involves and
perhaps the foregoing remarks will not appear so
enigmatical. You must, first of all, give some
idea of the habitation in which the soul dwells.
The man's personal appearance must somehow be
indicated. You can give his vital statistics, height,
weight, color of skin, facial contours, hair, chest
measurement; you can add a minute catalogue of
his articles of apparel, setting them forth with scientific accuracy; you can endow him with a cane,
an umbrella, an eye-glass; you can note his jewel-
lery. All this may take up pages of description,
but when you have written the items down you
have not proceeded very far in the accomplish-
ment of your purpose. Your model talks. He
says " Good morning " as you meet him, and
remarks that it is a fine day. He says many
other things, and you can put on paper all you
remember of what he has ever said. You observe him for several days and jot down all his
remarks. What you write you can add to the

vital statistics under a new heading: "Jenkins: I. How he looks. II. What he says." You may then go on to tell what he does habitually; what he eats and drinks, how he takes exercise, what papers he reads, how often he blows his nose. Having described his conversation, you can also speak of his walk under a third caption: "III. What he does." All this accomplished, you can put the notes together and hold him out to the reader triumphantly: "This is Jenkins; I have performed a work of art." Pardon, my friend, you have done nothing of the sort. You have not presented Jenkins at all. You evidently do not know him, or if you do, you have given us no intelligible idea of him.

Yet who does not recall instances of tales in which such a course is pursued? Page upon page, introducing a character with long, ambulatory description, full of adjectives of sonorous quality— the author evidently flattering himself, when he has got through, that he has painted a portrait. And the more minute the details are, the more realistic is the narrative said to be. But this is not realism, although many writers, from following the realistic method, err in just this way, because they do not understand that organic unity is the essence of realism.

It must be borne in mind that it is impossible to record all the particulars observable in any person. If, then, we simply collect all we can and stop when we get tired, it very likely will be the case that we have omitted the items which, if seized upon, would have rendered all the rest unnecessary. The salient, the characteristic features are the ones needed; and the power of the writer lies in his ability to indicate these in a few words of characterization, in an expression from the mouth of the person portrayed, in some act peculiarly and essentially his own. In actual contact with people, we never take our impressions by constantly dwelling upon details and adding them up. A rapid, selective, associative process goes on, by which a totality of impression is formed, certain features or actions being fastened upon as typical indicia of character. We, therefore, expect the literary artist to do for us what our own minds would do if we saw the original of the portrait. We want the living being, not a lot of chopped fragments placed in contiguity.

If these remarks have force with respect to the exhibition of a single character, they have still more weight as applied to the method of reproducing the relations of human beings in social life. A power of selection is absolutely necessary, or, instead of a clear and distinct picture, we shall have a monotonous, incoherent collection of unrelated facts. As M. Lemaitre well says: * " The artist, to transport his models into the romance or upon the stage, is *forced* to choose, to retain from

* " Les Contemporains ": Zola.

the reality only the characteristic traits and so to dispose of them as to cause the dominant character to appear saliently, whether it be of a society or of a single individual."

The reproduction of nature requires, therefore, much more than a cataloguing of particular items. But while this last will never produce a narrative which is realistic in any proper sense of the term, the process which the maker of the catalogue goes through is, I think, indispensable to true artistic reproduction. The trouble is, he too often gives us his rough notes, his studies, instead of the completed product to which we are entitled. Neither an individual character nor the "*milieu*"* can be successfully depicted without minute anatomical dissection, without study of models in every particular. The more profound, the more thorough, the more indefatigable that study, the greater the probability of success in the reproduction. The aim must be to see things as they are, not as we fancy they may be. This requires patient, careful, trained observation. It demands a well-developed capacity for generalization, including classification. It needs the highest cultivation of all the powers of association. The deepest analysis, the most comprehensive synthesis are alike requisite. He has a very superficial idea of the matter who supposes that we can see anything whatever in the world about us merely by opening

* Environment.

our eyes and allowing the light to form objects on the retina. This affords us nothing but kaleidoscopic pictures which are meaningless without the synthetical activity of the mind. For the simplest perceptions, memory, inference, imagination, and generalization are called into use. It is the exercise of these faculties that gives all their life to the objects we perceive.

The understanding of character cannot be effected by simple observation of other men and women as we see them in real life. Looks, words, acts, can only be interpreted by a reference to the author's own feelings, motives, desires. He reads the doings of others in the light of his own sentiments. Introspective analysis must go along with extrinsic observation. He can note what a person does under given circumstances, but he cannot comprehend and explain that action except by looking within his own consciousness. It thus happens that he must infuse his own personality even into that work which professes to be no more than a reproduction. There is always danger that he may do this to an extent too great; but if he looks within for the general and typical in human character and uses this as his measure, he will not fail.

In order to appreciate variations from his own standards and see clearly the operation of the countless subtle influences that determine conduct, the writer must have quick and ample sympathies. He must be able to put himself in the place of his characters, feel the pressure of their circumstances, observe the multifold impacts and counter-actions of environing forces. Their inner lives must not only be mirrored in his mind, but he must live those lives himself, be moved with their emotions and governed by their thoughts. When thus possessed, with his interest centred upon his model, he will behold the character as it is, he will seize upon the essential and reject the accidental; the things that otherwise would have escaped him are at once fastened upon, and when he is ready to write, the literary artist will find himself in the condition described by George Eliot in " Adam Bede," when " words came to me as tears come when the heart is full and we cannot prevent them." These words will be the right words, they will be clearly and distinctly descriptive; the portrait will stand out at last like a sculptured figure of Apelles, " full, and round, and fair." This and this only is realism worth relying upon.

It will hence be seen that for reproductive work in literary fiction that reproduces anything, very much the same processes are gone through, and the same powers of the mind called into exercise, as in creative art. It must be evident that without skill in reproduction, creation is not possible. The latter is recombination, and unless the elements can be reproduced with accuracy and fulness, there is little chance of a new unity being produced which signifies anything to the mind. Moreover, it is by the persistent, absorbing study of existing objects, of things and of men as they are, that the idealizing tendencies are stimulated and set free. Having a realizing sense of present woe, feeling sympathetically the pains of actual conditions, the desire for improvement develops ideals of such a betterment, the constructive activity of imagination suggests means for attaining it, and forms definite pictures of what joy it will bring when secured. It is only by understanding what is, by sympathy with sorrow arousing dissatisfaction in our minds, that creative intellect will give us the conception of something better.

A very profound thought is often suggested to me in connection with that picture by Raphael in the Vatican, called the " School of Athens." It is the thought of a teacher of mine,* who, calling attention to the two central figures of the picture —Plato looking and pointing upward, Aristotle with his gaze fixed upon the ground—remarks: " Philosophy, where its inspiration is highest and its investigations are deepest, reaches the same result, no matter in what direction it starts. Plato, beginning with the heavens, looked so comprehensively that he saw the earth shining in the light of the skies, and Aristotle, beginning with

* President J. H. Seelye, of Amherst College—Inaugural Address.

the earth, looked so deeply that he saw the heavens beneath it, the same heavens which Plato saw above." In like manner with art and the artist: he who fixes his eyes intently upon the earth, which at first seems to limit and obstruct his vision, if he continue his gaze with concentrated attention, will discover that it becomes transfigured, that the opaque inertness is interpenetrated with light and life, until at last, through its clarified form, he beholds also the shining of the stars.

I cannot but think this last method to be the true one, both for thought and art. Our business here is with the world about us. To deal with it, we must know it; and our knowledge is of the concrete, of the " things we see." The immortal and the eternal are only expressed to us in such terms, and I am sure the soul of nature will be found in the deep study of nature's work, rather than in any inspiring effort toward infinite knowledge, whose energy must needs be wasted in the vastness and *discreteness* * of a space which supplies no point of resistance, nothing upon which concentration is possible. Said Gogol: " I have studied life as it really is, not in dreams of the imagination; and thus I have come to a conception of Him who is the source of all life."

M. Zola is the great philosopher of the present realistic or naturalistic movement in fictitious lit-

* I use this term in a philosophical sense—discrete as opposed to concrete.

erature. In connection with what has been said, it may be well for us to learn from him how the realists themselves state their theory. According to M. Zola, realism is but the application of the scientific methods of observation and experiment in the construction of a work of literary art. In " Le Roman Expérimental," M. Zola takes as a text Claude Bernard's " Introduction à l'Étude de la Médicine expérimentale," and adopts precisely the method therein set forth as the method the "*romancier*" ought to pursue. This, to begin with, is the close and accurate observation of nature. But immediately a very important and significant addition is made ; namely, experiment. The reader is at once impelled to ask, What can "experiment" possibly mean in the romancer's art ? Certainly no one can take living human beings, put them into different environments at will, and see how they behave. We can do this with chemical elements, and to some extent with animals, but our power in this respect is sadly limited when we deal with men and women. What M. Zola means, therefore, must be something different. He explains, in the language of Bernard : " We give the name of *observer* to him who applies the processes of investigation, simple or complex, to the study of phenomena which he does not vary, and which he consequently receives as nature offers them to him. We give the name of *experimenter* to him who employs the processes of investigation, simple or complex, to vary or modify, in accordance with some purpose, the natural phenomena, and make them appear under circumstances or conditions in which nature does not present them." The observer finds "the relations which bind any phenomenon to its proximate cause," * or, in other words, determines the conditions necessary to the manifestation of this phenomenon. Then the experimenter inaugurates, institutes, a series of events in accordance with the laws of cause and effect discovered. He creates personages and incidents to develop naturally some idea, to illustrate some general fact which he has observed. This "idea of experiment carries with it the idea of modification. We set out indeed from true facts, which are our indestructible foundation ; but to reveal the mechanism of the facts we must have produced and directed the phenomena. There lies our part of invention, of genius in the work." "We ought to modify nature without emerging from nature when we employ in our romances the experimental method." "The problem is to know what a particular passion, acting in a particular environment and under particular circumstances, will produce, both as regards the individual and social interest ; and an experimental romance—'Cousine Bette,' for example (Balzac)—is simply the *procès-verbal* of the experi-

---

* This and the following quotations are in M. Zola's own words.

ment, which the romancer repeats under the eye
of the public. To sum up, the whole operation
consists in taking the facts of nature, then study-
ing the mechanism of the facts, treating them by
modifying according to circumstances and environment, without ever departing from the laws of
nature." " It is undeniable that the naturalistic
romance, as we understand it at present, is a true
experiment which the romancer makes upon man,
aiding it with observation."

It is quite apparent that the use of the term
experiment, as above, is unauthorized. The novelist does not, in any proper sense, perform ex-
periments. He does not, in fact, vary actual conditions, but only imagines them varied, deducing
certain conclusions on the supposition that they
are thus changed. In other words, he makes an
hypothesis, and, having settled his hypothetical
foundation or point of departure, he makes other
hypotheses conditioned thereon. There may be
found results in actual life which verify these and
enable us to formulate general truths about human nature. Again, such verification may not be
possible; but, whether or no, the process is one
of making suppositions and drawing inferences.
Now an hypothesis is a scientific ideal. It is a
fiction, conformable to experience and analogy,
suggested according to probabilities, but not yet
confirmed by more certain evidence. It is a product of the constructive powers of the intellect, a

work of the imagination; in fine, a development
of creative art. Realism, then, requires both reproduction and creation, and, according to M.
Zola, the latter would seem to be of the greater
importance.

Let us also at this point take account of the
opinions of M. de Maupassant, who is not so
much of a philosopher as M. Zola, but is a better
artist. He, however, has his theory with regard to
works of fiction, like the author of " Les Rougon-
Macquart," only he is more catholic. He does
not despise the idealist, who is in his judgment
really a poet, but he prefers the realistic or naturalistic method for prose fiction. He is a realist,
though not a bigoted one. In his view the romance of to-day writes "the history of the heart,
the soul, the intelligence, in the normal state. To
produce the effect at which he aims—that is to say,
the impression of simple reality—and to make
clear the artistic lesson which he wishes to draw
from it—that is, the true revelation of contemporary man to himself—he ought to employ
only those statements whose truth is unexception-
able and certain." But from the point of view of
the realists themselves,* their theory requires
some departure from that expressed by the words
"*Rien que la vérité et toute la vérité.*" † For, their

---

* I here slightly paraphrase the author's text in the preface of
" Pierre et Jean."

† " Nothing but the truth ; and the whole truth."

intention being to define the philosophy of certain
constant and evident facts of human nature, it is
necessary to correct the results of actual observation to accord with probabilities, since the true
sometimes is not probable. The true realist, then,
"if he be an artist, will seek, not to exhibit to us
a commonplace photograph of life, but to give us
a vision of it more complete, more striking, and
more authentic than the reality itself." Reproducing the truth, then, consists in giving a complete vision of the truth, following the natural
logic of the facts, and not transcribing them in
servile fashion in the "*pêle-mêle*" of their succession. "From these things I conclude that the
realists of talent ought rather to call themselves
Illusionists."

This is not very different from M. Zola's doctrine, though it is evident that M. de Maupassant
would sanction a wider departure from the standard of literal reproduction of nature than would
the author of "L'Assommoir." But both of them
insist, in theory, on the necessity for realism of selecting the facts to be recorded and of tracing out
by imagination and inference the supposed natural sequences of those facts. They tell us in one
breath to follow and to depart from nature. We
cannot help feeling a little puzzled, therefore, to
discover what is the ground of their quarrel with
the "idealists." Why talk about "naturalism" or
"realism," as if it were something new, or as if

it disclosed any new method in art? All artists who have succeeded have understood that it is necessary to study nature; that it will not answer the purpose to paint a cow on the hillside in the background of the picture so that it looks like a guinea-pig in a tree in the foreground. The masters of fiction at all periods have appreciated that they must draw their characters rightly and depict their scenes accurately. The one must be life-like, the other natural, and in accordance with probabilities and congruities. The fiction writer's art must necessarily be both reproductive and creative. We have just seen how creation is absolutely essential to reproduction; and how if we create we only recombine things that are produced for us in nature. According to the realists themselves, so-called naturalism does not indicate anything else beyond these two processes, both of which must always be employed and which are complementary to each other.

Thus, while we may agree with M. Zola that "realism" expresses a method, we fail to perceive how it declares a distinctive method, or one which does not appertain to all art. It must, then, be in the application somewhere that an issue is raised between realists on the one side and idealists or romantic novelists on the other.* Let us look to this a little.

---

* I do not see that there is use any longer for the division expressed by the word "classicism."

If a writer believes that he ought to study nature thoroughly, letting nothing escape him, he
will devote himself to the observation of details
and concentrate his attention upon minutiæ. Unless he is careful he will find himself absorbed in
these items. He will collect a multitude of small
unities without seeing the larger unity into which
they might be combined. These details will be
viewed as through a magnifying glass, which en-
larges their importance and at the same time nar-
rows the field of vision. There is danger that the
writer will forget that the reader can only become
interested by the same course of laborious application that the author has pursued, losing sight
of the fact that the reader has not the inspiring
purpose which animates the chronicler. The latter will work to produce his story; the former will
not work to read it. Now we find that the realists exemplify the foregoing remarks very generally and characteristically, none more so than
the author of "Les Rougon-Macquart." He
declares that the writer of a romance " is not a
moralist, but an anatomist who contents himself
with telling what he finds in the human corpse."*
He says that the formula of the naturalistic method
in literature is the same as that of the sciences,
particularly physiology. It is a searching inquest
into the vital, organic facts of individual and so-

---

* "Les Romanciers Naturalistes."

cial life in all their manifestations.* So in his novels he heaps up details in masses which are appalling. His net gathers in the small and great. Collecting everything, he must needs get many things that are characteristic and striking. M. Lemaitre remarks of him : † "One of the virtues of M. Zola is indefatigable and patient energy. He sees clearly concrete things, all the exterior of life, and he has a peculiar faculty of describing that which he sees. His is the power of retaining and accumulating a greater quantity of details than any other of the same school, and he does this coldly, tranquilly, without weariness or disgust, and giving to everything the same even prominence and accent. The result is that the unity of each picture lies no more as with the classic writers in the subordination of the details (seldom numerous) to the whole, but, if I may say so, in their interminable monochromatic quality."

The public, said Stendhal in one of his letters, wants a greater number of "*petit faits vrais*, upon a passion or a situation in life." He himself tried to satisfy them in his romances, and still more so did his great follower Balzac, though I doubt if the mind of the latter was occupied with the thought of any *magna instauratio* in literature so much as of himself doing a monumental work. But Balzac exhibits the acme of realism in por-

---

* "Le Roman Naturaliste."   † "Les Contemporains."

trait painting, as M. Zola does in presenting the
" *milieu*." The record of two thousand of these
figures depicted with the utmost fineness of analysis, with item upon item of traits, characteristics,
habits, appearances, entitles him to be called, in the
language of Taine, as next after Shakespeare, our
greatest magazine of documents on human nature.
" In Balzac," observes Henry James,* " every one
who is introduced is minutely described ; if the
individual is to say but three words he has the
honors of a complete enumeration." Like Stendhal, the author of the " Comédie Humaine " fully
believed "*qu'il n'est point de sensibilité sans détails.*" †

The naturalistic romancer who is thoroughly
possessed by his theory, in his anxiety to be faithful to nature, even to the extent of recording the
revelations of the microscope upon anatomy, will
be prone to regard it as his duty to note down the
" *détails scabreux.*" Inasmuch as there are many
facts of individual and social life of which people
take as little account as possible, which are not
mentioned frequently in conversation, and upon
which the minds of most persons are not fond of
dwelling, novelists in general have not thought
proper to allude to them in their stories, or if they
deem it necessary to make allusion, they have
done so rather by suggestion and with a light

---

* " French Poets and Novelists."   † Stendhal : "Son Journal."

touch. The "naturalist," however, because of this very reticence, is at once impressed with a sense of incompleteness and empiricism in the works of such romancers, and with a solemn and stern sense of obligation proceeds unflinchingly to his task of remedying this deficiency. He does not consider whether or not the unmentionable objects or incidents are necessary to the plan of his work. The fact that in real life they may be present or may occur is enough to render it incumbent upon him to introduce them in the story. Hence they are presented with the same fulness and minuteness of description as is everything else, despite the probable shrinking of the reader. Thus, say the realists, humanity is depicted as it is and the whole truth is told.

This same relentless determination to seek and reveal "*toute la vérité*" influences also the choice of subjects which for reasons like those mentioned in the last paragraph have not been fully exploited. M. Zola thus takes possession of a field which before his time has not been at all thoroughly worked. The phase of life chosen, together with his naturalistic theory, hence compel the presentation to the reader of a great deal that is malodorous, filthy, and disgusting. Ordure, putrescence, beastliness must necessarily appear. The smell of the butcher-shop, the sewer, the markets, the gin-mill, the barn-yard is made real to us, or the author aims to make it so. "Naturalism" is even

carried so far that in " La Terre " an entire chapter is devoted to one of the most obscene and offensive incidents of intestinal and sphincterial action. Similarly, by writers like M. de Maupassant,
the sexual appetite in all its developments, its impulses, its vagaries, becomes the theme to be an-
alyzed and illustrated in the most minute particulars. So far are all these ideas of naturalism
carried that we are quite disposed to agree with
M. Paul Bourget in his characterization of the
"realists " as " the fanatics of modern literature ! "

The last-named critic has suggested another characteristic tendency of current realism,* namely,
to produce a " mediocrity of heroes, a systematic diminution of the plot, a nearly complete
suppression of dramatic facts." He instances
" L'Education Sentimentale " of Flaubert as the
best-defined model of this sort of romance. To
this tendency I referred some pages back. M. Zola
justifies it, as well as he can, in his discussion.
The natural-history method has no need of plot.
" A novel was formerly a record of adventure ; it
is now a study of character. It was formerly objective dealing with the actions of men and their
outer surroundings. It is now subjective dealing
with the mental state, the impulses and passions,
the motives and principles of men, and using
events simply as the machinery of the story." †

* " Réflexions sur l'Art du Roman."
† W. L. Alden, in the *Galaxy*.

Inasmuch as the most are not cast in the heroic mould, ordinary people appear as affected by their different environments. The extraordinary is the more improbable, both as to characters and incidents. The greater portion of the situations in actual life are not dramatic, and the more we depart from what is common and recognized, the more certain is there to be an air of unreality about the narrative which is not congruous with the scientific standard. It should be said that writers who are in many respects realistic, in others oppose many of the tendencies of realism of which I have spoken and shall speak. Balzac certainly has created some very extraordinary characters, abnormal and sometimes bizarre, not at all common as specimens of the human race. But still it is no doubt true that naturalism has abated if not abolished the hero, diminished the plot-interest, and turned the attention away from the strictly romantic, using the old sense of the word.

Another application of the realistic idea is especially insisted on by M. Zola. That which it is above all necessary to lay emphasis upon is the impersonal character of the method. Personal authority is at a minimum. We are held to an exposition of *how* things come to pass, not *why* they occur. We, the writers, are observers, and we should assume a strictly scientific attitude. We need not trouble others with our own notions of what ought to be. Our own views, our approval and disapproval, our wishes, are quite irrelevant. Our work is scientific criticism, declaratory of what is. Our authority is only the facts. In fine, the writer should keep himself and his personality wholly in the background. Balzac, indeed, was a most incorrigible offender against this canon of fiction-composition. He insists on philosophizing, moralizing, preaching everywhere, in season and out of season. Nor is this all. He colors everything with his own biases and prejudices. He cannot be respectful to anybody he doesn't like. As Henry James says, " He hated the bourgeoisie with an unmitigable hatred ; and more than most of his class, he hated the provincial." Thus to him the world was the world seen through his colored glasses—a fact which calls to mind the quotations with which this chapter was opened. That was realistic which agreed with his " illusion " of life. But whatever we may think of M. Zola's practice, his theory requires the elimination of personal prejudice. The naturalistic romancer must be an impartial observer and " experimenter," aiming only to reveal the truth without comment.

Enough has been now said to enable us to make a generalization which, very likely, has already suggested itself to the reader. These specific applications of the doctrine of naturalism as made by the chief of the " naturalists " all conduce to the reduction of art to science. Their principal aim is to give us knowledge instead of æsthetic pleasure.

They eliminate the artistic for the benefit of the scientific. If everything is to be subordinated to actuality, there is no room for ideality, except in the form of hypothesis. M. Zola not only admits this, but he urges on the extreme consummation. " Enlarge still more the *rôle* of the experimental sciences; extend it even to the study of the passions and the portrayal of manners. You have then our romances which seek the causes and explain them, which collect documents on human nature, by which one can become master both of man and his environment in such a way as to be able to develop the good elements and exterminate the bad. We do a work identical with that of the scientists." *

No one can possibly appreciate the importance of science more highly than I do, but I am wholly unable to see why art is not desirable to cultivate for its own sake. That our education should be primarily and fundamentally scientific I cannot doubt. And if men are willing to devote their whole lives to the scientific study of any of the phenomena of the universe, cosmological, biological, or sociological, confining their thought to details and seeking knowledge by close analysis, they have a noble ambition and are doing an honorable and praiseworthy work. But why should we, therefore, say that the imaginative or creative

---

* " Lettres à la Jeunesse."

faculty, which is especially fitted to enable us to
transcend the world of the natural and real, should
be limited in its exercise to scientific, closely ver-
ifiable hypothesis? If we are able to conceive a
centaur, why should we be restrained from doing
so because no centaurs have yet been found? If
the idealizing capacity brings pleasure, joy, delight, why not so employ it? One would almost
think the naturalistic philosophers were becoming
ascetics! Must artists die that savants may live?
Because our work is on the ground, in the heat
and dust, may we never free ourselves, soar aloft
on the wings of the morning, and knock at the
portals of the day before it dawns?

In the first place, it should be seen that scientific fiction is, strictly speaking, a contradiction in
terms. So far forth as fiction is science it ceases
to be fiction ; so far forth as science is fictitious
it ceases to be science. If science be all in all,
would it not be better to leave out the fictitious
element altogether from literature and devote ourselves to exact descriptions of actual persons,
types, and conditions? We could greatly improve
history and biography by the more faithful employment of the naturalistic method. Or, if this
were dangerous with respect to biographical accounts, we might still study real individuals, using
fictitious names, or initials like X and Y, the
algebraic symbols. Again, are not tables of actual
observations, like those of Herbert Spencer's

" Descriptive Sociology," much better for scientific purposes? And if they were extended to
English or French society of the appropriate
periods, would they not be far preferable to
Disraeli and George Eliot or to the " Comédie
Humaine"? Would not M. Zola have realized
the ends he professes to seek more completely if
he had given us his notes upon which he built
up " Pot-Bouille" and " La Terre" rather than
the books themselves? We have shown how his
" experiment" is nothing but hypothesis. To be
truly scientific, should not this all be left out and
the exact results of observation be given clearly
and concisely? What need of Buteaus, of Nanas,
of Paulines, of Etiennes, to be manufactured
with so much trouble, when at the end they are
only supposititious and hypothetical characters?
Better turn to biography and history and plain
realistic portraits of lunatics, monsters, loafers,
drunkards, harlots, as they abound in actual life,
have them labelled and identified, and put away
in some collection, or published with the transac-
tions of some sociological society. The members
of the Parisian Association for Mutual Autopsy
might make themselves useful even before their
decease by practising the naturalistic method of
analysis upon each other's characters!

In Chapter III. I endeavored to show that there
is a scientific value to the novel and in what it
consists. But it will be seen that this value is a

substitutive one. We cannot do better, from force of circumstances. Because we have no societies for Mutual Ante-mortem Dissection, and because there are few Rousseaus who are willing to be frank and explicit in their confessions, we cannot exhibit character in its various forms, except under the guise of fiction. Since there are kings, popes, and popular sentiments, we cannot always portray social, political, and religious conditions as facts of science. Moreover, the question of interest comes in. Dry statistics will not be read. An artistic clothing is an immense help in imparting knowledge. The romance, therefore, is indeed a vehicle for teaching science; but never can it become the chief or the best means for inculcating scientific knowledge. To attempt to make it such would result in destroying its æsthetic value, which would in turn take away its value for scientific purposes.

If we countenance fiction at all, we do so primarily because of its æsthetic value. It is a work of art and it must respect the canons of art. Otherwise it becomes a confused and useless mixture, neither one thing nor the other. It is crude or imperfect science and it is poor art. It must appeal to the æsthetic sense, never losing sight of that primal condition of artistic work, the elimination of the disagreeable. It must cater to our appreciation of beauty, harmony, variety in unity, symmetry, proportion, grace, delicacy, congruity. Since it must needs be a product of human constructiveness, the first aim should be to make it, as such, a good piece of work, not a bad one.

There is another important consideration which extremists in naturalism are apt to overlook. If we are to follow nature, study the workings of the human mind and its results in all their development, if we are to pass by none of the passions, impulses, desires, dispositions which issue in human action in such great variety, why should we omit the *furor scribendi* and its products in creative art? If a person has a mania for creating Mephistos and Calibans, for describing a Dantean Inferno or Paradiso in prose fiction, for giving life in the world of literature to a Frankenstein or a Seraphita—beings that never were and, so far as we are able to see, never can be—why are not such productions of scientific interest as exhibiting the power of mental forces? If no better, the work itself may be a most valuable indication of pathological conditions. It enables us to study the human mind and character just as well, oftentimes more satisfactorily, than if we direct our observation to the relations of conduct between man and man. And as for the writer, how can any one be more realistic than when he is giving free expression to the creative activities of his own mind, showing forth the power and indeed the life of his very soul in the exuberant play of fancy and imagination which artistic liberty always allows and stimulates? M. Zola and his *confrères*

do not seem to understand that whatever we may
say of the propriety of making the romance "impersonal" as to the author, it never can be done.
Why? Because the romance is a work of art. It
is a constructive product of a human mind, a personality which comes before the reader and appeals to him as such. This is always an element
of the interest, as we noted in Chapter I., and
again at the close of Chapter V. The story or
romance is a means of communication between
human beings. It is something which the author
imparts to his readers of his own perception,
thought, and feeling. We cannot get rid of this
personal element if we try. There remains always
at least the interest in the skill, the ingenuity, the
cleverness of the contriver, the artificer, the one
who conquers difficulties, of which I have several
times spoken. M. Zola may pride himself upon
his impersonality in the "Rougon-Macquart"
novels, but he deceives himself mightily if he
thinks the world will not, in addition to other interests, look at them, study them, criticise them,
as pieces of work turned out by the workman
Emile Zola, and as revelations of his own mind
and character. We do not like to have the personality of the author thrust upon us, but nevertheless we always take note of it. In the words of
M. David-Sauvageot:* "We love to divine, behind

* "Le Réalisme et le Naturalisme," etc.

the veil of dramatic fiction, a distinct personality which makes effort neither to disclose nor conceal itself." There is a great deal of force, too, in the following remarks of Véron,* though they must not be taken too universally and absolutely: "The degree of reality which a work of art exhibits is of æsthetic importance only because it enables us to measure the power of penetration necessary to seize it, and the force of imagination which has permitted its reproduction with that distinctness which we admire." Again: " When we follow the development of the characters of Tartuffe, of Avare, of Cousine Bette, of Marneffe, that which interests us, æsthetically speaking, . . . is the profundity of observation, thanks to which Molière and Balzac have been able to penetrate to the heart of their characters; and, above all, the power of depiction by which they are able to make them come forth into the light of the stage or the romance, and make of them living beings. That which we admire in the characters is not themselves, it is the genius which has created them."

Although there are some minor points which might be made in addition, we are now in a position to see clearly, I think, that if we attempt to make " realism " or " naturalism " a shibboleth of fiction-composition, we shall be in danger of suicidally perverting a true and useful method when

---

* " L'Esthétique," Part I., ch. vi.

properly applied, so far as to greatly and unwarrantably limit the sphere of romantic and creative
literature, to restrict it unduly within that sphere,
and even to threaten its entire extinction. This
perversion has gone far already ; and it is well to
call a halt in the march of naturalistic ideas in the
world of art, not for the purpose of going back to
the old romanticism, but with the view of deter-
mining our position, seeing the end from the beginning, and ascertaining whither our progress tends.

After this long discussion, then, let us get before
our minds succinctly, by way of summary, the uses
and limitations of the naturalistic method. If it
be regarded as a mode of discipline and prepara-
tion, it is absolutely indispensable. No one can
be a truly great artist in anything who is not able
to reproduce nature as she is. For—if the reader
will pardon reiteration—our material for construction is nothing else but what our experiences of
nature give us. If we desire to create we can only
rearrange and rehabilitate. In order to execute,
to *do* anything, we must *know*. Let us remember
what Ruskin says in " Modern Painters " : * "All
qualities of execution, properly so called, are influenced by, and in a great degree dependent on,
a far higher power than that of mere execution—
knowledge of truth. For exactly in proportion as
an artist is certain of his end, will he be swift and

---

* Part I., sec. ii., ch. ii.

simple in his means; and as he is accurate and
deep in his knowledge will he be refined and precise in his touch. The first merit of manipulation,
then, is that delicate and ceaseless expression
of refined truth which is carried out to the last
touch, and shadow of a touch, and which makes
every hair's breadth of importance, and every gra-
dation full of meaning." Therefore, it is of the
utmost importance for the sake of expression
both that the author have something to express
and know that something. Storing his mind with
material, if he comprehends through and through
that which he has observed, he so much the more
increases his power to utilize successfully whatever he has gathered.

Furthermore, as we also learned, completeness
and thoroughness of observation is a powerful aid
to the development of the creative powers. The
imagination is thereby stimulated, strengthened,
and trained. By following nature, we at last become nature's master. Again, to apply the words
of Ruskin—these for the admonition of young artists: "They should keep to quiet colors, grays
and browns; and . . . should go to nature in
all singleness of heart, and walk with her labori-
ously and trustingly, having no other thoughts
but how to penetrate her meaning, and remember her instruction, rejecting nothing, . . .
scorning nothing. . . . Then, when their mem-
ories are stored and their imaginations fed,

and their hands firm, let them take up the scarlet and the gold, give the reins to their fancy,
and show us what their heads are make of.
We will follow them wherever they choose to
lead ; we will check at nothing ; they are then our
masters, and are fit to be so."

These last precepts show forth the heritage of
the true artist.   They admonish us not to sacrifice
our birthright for a mess of pottage.   They tell us
that the " experimental method " is a means, not
an end.   We must not make the mistake of sup-
posing that the study of nature consists only in
an enumeration of nature's phenomena.   Nor can
we impose upon the world by giving it our
sketches and studies as the *finale* of art.   The
use of " observation and experiment " is to enable
us the better to employ our faculties.   In that
employment we may introduce new beings into
nature, we may exaggerate nature, we may even
transcend nature, as Michael Angelo, Shakespeare,
and Balzac did.   By following her we have simply
trained our selective and constructive powers to
enter into the vast unknown, and call forth its
spirits by our words of command.

Hence " naturalism " never must be allowed to
limit our creative activity, but only minister unto
it, chastening it to enable us to give substance
rather than shadow. It must not chain genius
down.   It must not restrict its selection of subjects, nor must it absolutely control its treatment

of them. It may lay the foundation, furnish the brick and stone and the mortar, but not the architecture of the building. The ideal must supervene and supply the guiding hand, the scheme, the form. In Bulwer's words,* " Art, from all forms of the positive is ever seeking to extract the ideal." " The base of art is in the study of nature; not to imitate, but first to select and then to combine from nature those materials into which the artist can breathe his own vivifying idea." Says Goethe in " Wilhelm Meister," of the true artists: " Pausing at some standpoint of ideal perception, they let the variety of life pass under their eyes, and translate its meanings into the new language of their genius." Let us listen also to Mr. Robert Louis Stevenson : † " The whole secret is, that no art does compete with life." " Let the writer choose a motive, whether of character or ·passion, . . . and allow neither himself nor any character in the course of the dialogue to utter one sentence that is not part and parcel of the business of the story, or the discussion of the problem involved." " And as the root of the whole matter, let him bear in mind that his novel is not a transcript of life to be judged by its exactitude, but a simplification of some side or point of life, to stand or fall by its significant simplicity."

M. David-Sauvageot, in the work before quoted

---

* " Caxtoniana."   † *Longman's Magazine.*

from,* has, to my mind, indicated the important
service performed by contemporary realism.   He
esteems its great value to lie in the reaction which
it has inaugurated against the arbitrary conventions of degenerate classic and of romantic art.   In
this he is, no doubt, quite right.   It has the value
of a protestation, a reformation.   The conventions
against which it is a reaction were, as he says, fashions controlled by the times and surviving simply
because they were fashions, after their producing
causes had ceased to act.   The world, to the reader
of former days, was only the " *milieu* " of princes
and grand seigneurs, of warriors, of demi-gods, of
palaces and castles, of personal combats, of Ho-
meric and feudalistic deeds.   These conventions
were imposed by the exigencies of public opinion,
by neglect of the constant evolution going on in
nature, thereby giving too great a rigidity to art ;
by a disposition to impose the processes of one
particular art upon all, and to separate utterly
art from nature, according to Goethe's principle as
De Quincey declares it : " Art is art, because it is
not nature."   Against these hard-and-fast principles of artistic production a powerful protest was
necessary.   This has certainly been delivered by
the naturalistic writers, and very efficaciously.   It
is in truth a manifestation of the æsthetic impulse
demanding freedom for itself ; and in obtaining

---

* " Le Réalisme et le Naturalisme," etc.

this it made possible and actual a better art; for "It is only in the conditions of an absolute freedom that any real art can be done."* Let the liberators then be careful lest they impose upon us a new tyranny, whose trammels will make necessary a counter-movement in the interest of artistic liberty and progress.

Indeed, M. David-Sauvageot thinks that realism has only prepared the way for a new and dominating idealism. He quotes Fustel de Coulanges to the effect that "there is need of volumes of analysis to give a line of synthesis." As, from 1600 to 1636, French literature abounded in a fertile confusion of essays and researches, out of whose condensation came the *Cid*, so may we anticipate that the realism of Flaubert and of M. Zola will ultimate in "an idealism less profound perhaps, but more free and more comprehensive than that of a Molière and a Racine."

Upon the whole, then, we are forced to the conclusion that realism could not, if it would, dispense with creativeness, save by abolishing art in reducing it to science; but that, if rightly understood, it is of great value in making strong, clear, and life-like the products of creation. Furthermore, while it is at the foundation of all reproductive art, its methods will not even there supersede the necessity of employing a selective process which

---

* Ouida : *North American Review.*

6

is determined by ideals. In all the recent discussions the true relations of realism and idealism to
each other have not been better expressed than
they were by Frances Power Cobbe * twenty-five
years ago, in estimating the elements of value in
creative and reproductive art respectively. She
says: " The value of creative art is determined by
two conditions: first, by the extent and fulness
with which the artist has received the divine revelation of beauty in nature; secondly, by the faithfulness with which he has recorded what he has
received. The value of reproductive art is determined by the intrinsic excellence of the work he
chooses to reproduce; secondly, by the extent to
which he has reproduced in fresh form and not
merely copied the work in question; thirdly, by
the perfection of his own achievement as itself a
work of art, judged independently from the original."

Since we discover, therefore, that realism only
endows us with a method to be used under the
guidance of ideals formed by the synthetic and
selective activities of the mind, we have still to
search for a principle of selection. We are thus
thrown back upon the question of interest and the
interaction of scientific, moral, and æsthetic motives. We can then understand the meaning of
the two passages quoted at the very beginning of

---

* " The Hierarchy of Art," 1865.

this chapter, which are not comprehensible on the theory that the ends of art are satisfied by observing and presenting everything and anything that appears in nature. In that case whatever is portrayed should appear equally realistic to everybody, if it be a faithful copy. But the reader as well as the writer selects, out of natural phenomena, objects which assimilate with his own character and life. He thus to a degree makes his own world, and that artist appears realistic to him who exhibits his own "illusion." Hence the explanation of the strange contrarieties in criticisms of artistic work, one praising and another condemning; one believing the production fanciful, another esteeming it remarkably true to life. It is evident, then, that we must consider further, and in greater detail, the various objects of interest and causes of interest which give popularity and success to the story that brings them before the mind. This we shall proceed to do in the succeeding chapters.

CHAPTER VII.

THE EXHIBITION OF POWER.

A MANIFESTATION of great power in nature always arrests attention, whether it be simple force or that to which a moral quality, beneficent or maleficent, attaches. This is true not only in that sense of the word which implies passive superiority, but also in the signification of energy and activity. Again, the effect is produced both by brute, massive strength and by cunning, subtle skill. Whatever shows great material, vital, passional, or intellectual force commands attention.

Experience is made up of a succession of actions and reactions. The thousand-and-one movements in the world about us, of air, of light, of gravity, of animals, of human beings in the ordinary course of their avocations, however, do not and cannot all impress themselves upon us. The most of them are not noticed at all. There must be something extraordinary, outside of the common flow of phenomena, to occupy our thought or divert it. Novelty itself will seize the attention, but the continuance of the impression is conditioned by the quantity of the sensation, which itself depends upon the stimulus already acting, or other coincident attractions.

Accounts of great convulsions of nature will, therefore, interest a reader if they are so given as to awaken to some degree the same emotions that the spectator would have were he present at the actual occurrence. These feelings must be very much weaker, and in consequence of that weakness other emotions come into play which would not have appeared in the original experience. No doubt a simple description of the destruction of Pompeii, if well done, would hold the reader, even if the relations that ruin bore to individual characters did not appear. Historical accounts of this sort are always interesting. When, therefore, an interest in human beings, as affected by the natural disturbance, is superadded, as in Bulwer's "Last Days," a powerful impression is produced. It may be well to analyze a little the interest thus experienced with the view of ascertaining the generic effects of the exhibition of power in nature.

In Bulwer's novel, just mentioned, the overwhelming of the city is the culmination, there being after it only a postscript chapter, " wherein all things cease"—especially the story. The ancient city is reconstructed and described, together with the manners and customs of the inhabitants; a little world of characters is created whose fortunes are to be followed, and in whom an interest is aroused quite independently of the *dénouement.* They might have been disposed of without ruining the whole place, and still we should have been tolerably well satisfied. When, however, the catastrophe arrives, how are we affected? In such manner as if we were there, had partly seen what happened and some one had told us the rest. The picture of the city and the volcano is in our minds and thoughts of the people whom we knew.

In the first place, fear controls the situation. Our senses are affected by the tremendous phenomena, the lurid light, the frightful noise, the choking odors, the incessant activity, the violent disintegration and destruction going on. These things paralyze us for the moment, at least, and we are thrown into a receptive state in which our own activities are abated. If, now, we were actually on the spot this inaction would soon be succeeded by thoughts of escape, plans and movements to that end. But when once in a position of safety, we gaze upon the eruption and witness its effects, the emotions of fear subside and are superseded by others of a different character. In place of a depression of vitality there comes an exaltation of it. We describe our feelings by the terms *Sense of Grandeur, of Sublimity.* We ally ourselves with a producing cause of what we see, think of ourselves as putting forth strength and also performing great results. We enter sympathetically into the succession of phenomena. We are lifted up into the region of a greater power and are filled with the buoyancy of an exalted life. Impressed at first by fear, our minds are afterward pervaded by an accretion of potent vitality which dominates, reduces, and casts out fear. The emotions thus arising are truly æsthetic. We do not suffer pain either physically or sympathetically. Pain is eliminated, and what the mind dwells upon are movements which develop feelings the reverse of disagreeable. If associations do bring up painful thoughts they are suspended by just the same process as before, and their irruption only serves to enhance the resultant pleasure.

A similar effect is produced by the more ordinary operation of natural forces. The lightning, the wind, the waves are often sublime. In many of these cases the fresh tonic air, invigorating and stimulating, directly inspires the feeling of strength. The sunlight, too, is in the most marked degree the cause of sensations of increased vitality. All the various movements of the air, the earth, the waters, awaken emotions of power in the beholder. In realistic description this pleasure is reproduced in the reader. It is precisely because of such an emotional stimulus that we enjoy passages like the following in the first chapter of Mr. William Black's "Princess of Thule": "From out of the lowering southwest fierce gusts of wind were driving up volumes and flying rags of clouds, and sweeping onward, at the same time, the gathering waves that fell hissing and thundering on the shore." Or those of which here is a sample from "Wanda," by Ouida: "There is such abundance of rushing water, of deep grass, of endless shade, of forest trees, of heather and pine, of torrent and tarn; . . . and the earth seems so green and *fresh*, and silent and *strong*." *

In the contemplation of mountains we have power impressed upon us also. Ruskin remarks, in "Modern Painters": † "Mountains are to the rest of the body of the earth what violent muscular action is to the body of man. The muscles and tendons of its anatomy are, in the mountain, brought out with fierce and convulsive energy, full of expression, passion, and strength. . . . The fiery peaks, which, with heaving bosoms and exulting limbs, with the clouds drifting like hair from their bright foreheads, lift up their Titan hands to heaven, saying, ' I live for ever.' " This is no meaningless rhetoric. It expresses most profound truth, and is an explanation of a primary influence nature has over us. We seek life—conservation, development of vital power—and wherever there is manifested power in nature we sympathize with it, we seek to drink of it, assimilate it, and feel it coursing in our veins. We even

---

* Italics mine.   † Part II., sec. iv., ch. i.

personify, and it seems to bring us near to a source of all power, from which we can renew our flagging energies. "The voice of thy thunder was in the heaven; the lightning lightened the world; the earth trembled and shook. Thy way is in the sea and thy path in the great waters." "I will lift up mine eyes unto the hills, *from whence cometh my help*."

But it is quite certain, as Mr. Walter Besant says,* that "the very first rule in fiction is that the human interest must absolutely absorb everything else;" and if power manifested in nature inanimate arouses an æsthetic emotion through sympathy, how inevitable that it should do so when displayed by human beings, with whom a personal sympathy is possible! The ideal of the perfection of one's own self, physically and mentally, which every one has, seems then to be realized, and our minds are filled with admiring joy as we behold. Who, in reading Homer's "Hymn to Apollo," for example, is not permeated with a consciousness of exhaustless strength lifting him up and making him feel as if he were breathing in the breath of eternal life? Thus the hero comes to be an object of primary interest in human society, and consequently in fictitious representations of it.

Power can be exhibited in many ways, and this

---

* " Art of Fiction."

very sympathy, which is necessary to our interest in its manifestations, has an important moderating and regulating effect upon our appreciation. People in every age mark out channels in which effort can be put forth, and beyond which it is useless. They form their ends according to existing conditions. A man is great who is strong in those particulars in which strength is needed. An Achilles in a modern community would be rated about on a par with a prize-fighter. Ulysses also would serve very well in that capacity. On the other hand, Lord Beaconsfield or Metternich would not have been eminent in Athenian society. The environment, the state of civilization, the limitations of activity by circumstances, determine the form in which greatness must appear, if at all.

The romancer, however, can construct a tale which exemplifies the heroism of an age long past ; and if he be skilful in portraying the appropriate " *milieu*," his story will be read. It will be praised because it is well done, and also because of the general fact that great deeds and qualities are intrinsically interesting ; but his circle of readers will be a somewhat limited one, and he will find critics complaining that his romance is dull and artificial. Then it is rarely the case that an author, imbued with the ideas and incidents of one generation, can reproduce satisfactorily to himself or anybody else the manners and deeds of a by-gone time. Nor will he be moved to try, save in exceptional instances. Hence, the fashion of the fictitious literature of any period is set by the conditions of thought and life in that period, and the best work is done according to that fashion.

Human power has been shown in history very largely in conflict between men. Although its methods have totally changed, war has not ceased to absorb people's thoughts and excite their feelings. In the shock of battle power is shown in two principal ways—the one in triumph and victory, the other in resistance and endurance. Both of these command admiration. The crushing of an adversary elicits our plaudits for the conqueror, while we cannot withhold our favor from him who has made an obstinate fight, but at last is forced to succumb. Yet our sympathies will always be with one of the combatants rather than with the other, and the elation at the success of the one we support causes us to forget or to dwell little upon the valor of the defeated. There are two series of impressions made upon him who is the witness of actual warfare. He is filled with satisfaction at the success of his cause, or his own deeds in the face of great dangers and trials, and he is horrified and sickened at the carnage, the suffering, the devastation. Which of these will be in the ascendant will depend upon his own make-up. In order to be a good soldier, however, there must be a callousness to suffering, a weakness of sympathy, which makes him glory in victory and mind little about the distressful side of warfare. In addition, there is very often, as remarked in our first chapter, a positive thirst for blood, which makes men delight in the sufferings of others, and even to take pleasure in inflicting pain. This ferocity of the wild beast has by no means been extinguished in human nature.

Now, the novelist in describing a battle may systematically lead the reader's mind along such a course as to fasten the attention upon the movements of success and failure, of victory and defeat, upon the heroic deeds ultimating in triumph, exciting all the enthusiasm called forth by the display of power in action, without allowing any reflection upon the butchery, the woe, the horror of the conflict. Walter Scott's tournaments, as in "Ivanhoe," furnish good samples of this for single combats, and Mr. Rider Haggard, in his South African adventures, for battles between armies. Such descriptions would not be called "realistic." But they comply with one of the chief canons of æsthetic pleasure, namely, that the disagreeable be eliminated. The majority of readers do not want to have the carnage vividly represented. They want the effects of rapid, brilliant, startling movement, the imposing charge, the overthrow of squadrons, the music of bands, and the hurrahs of victory. If they are told that men are mowed down like grass before the scythe, the thought exhilarates them as a natural step in the progress to the event, inasmuch as they do not realize in their feelings that anybody is hurt in the operation of mowing.

If, on the other hand, the writer chooses to be " realistic"—that is, realistic on the other side of the picture—and gives full account of the horrible wounds, the shrieks of agony, the smell of blood, the brutal onslaughts, the presence of death and despair, his narrative may interest, but from an entirely different principle. The interest is no longer from an exhibition of power. It may be that of the moralist, of which we shall speak by and by. Or it may be delight in blood and cruelty which demonstrates the tiger in human nature. The soldier of whom we just spoke, who is merely callous, will not be pleased by such a recital. Those are the things he seeks to overlook as well in actual battle as in the description. It is the one who pants " for the dreadful privilege to kill " * who takes pleasure in such particulars. They arouse, and to some extent gratify, the predatory lust. " Even in the midst of compassion," observes Montaigne, † " we feel within I know not what tart-sweet titillation of malicious pleasure in seeing others suffer ; children even have the same feeling." This introduces us to the whole subject of representation of the brutal and cruel,

---

* Horace, Sat. X., 96.   † " Essais," III., c. i.

which belongs rather to the category of suffering than of power. It is well for us, however, to note here the fact that connected with the exercise of destructive power there is an original pleasure, which is distinctively that of the carnivorous animal in killing its prey. It is shown in Bill Sykes of Dickens, in many of the characters and incidents of Roderick Random and Peregrine Pickle, and the novels of that period ; in Mr. Rider Haggard's Umslopogaas, in Mr. Stevenson's Hyde, and also in some of the scenes of Tolstoï's " War and Peace."

From this element of bloodthirstiness exhibi‚ tions of constructive power are free, though the same fatal effects may follow from disregard of the pain of others, as in cases of an overweening and selfish ambition. But in these instances the sympathy arises from the greatness of accomplish-ment, the attainment of magnificent ends, the sur-passing of serious obstacles, the triumph over difficulties. Hence our interest in the founders of empires, the liberators of peoples, the self-made men, the inventors, the great philanthropists. For the last-named, however, admiration does not spring wholly from sympathy with the achieve-ments as such, but from their beneficent character, their social value, their utility. Yet this altruistic regard is never essential to the interest. The development of a selfishness, able in securing its own ends, is just as sure to hold the attention, because it exhibits capacity and superiority. Becky Sharp* is certainly one of the characters of fiction that will endure, and it is not virtuous self-abnegation that appears as the prominent feature of her career. Again, the successful spoliation of Cousin Pons† strikes us as exceedingly clever, and we even detect ourselves entering into the plot with the conspirators and suggesting how we would do the thing if we were the actors. This is simply the interest in skilful activity, in contrivance, inventiveness, which obtains whether the end be diabolical or divine.

We shall not consider in this place how this last interest is nullified or counteracted, further than to say that it is by moral feeling. But even if our disapproval is strong, the story will occupy our mind if it be artistically told, with the unpleasant side of the events well-concealed or minified. When, however, the plan of the tale is to overwhelm, crush, or punish this able wickedness by a *vis major* of retributive justice, it may be important to the effect to set forth saliently and in detail the enormity of the villany, in order to make the triumph of the good seem greater.

As connected with the exhibition of skill and clever control of means for given ends, we must not lose sight of the fact that the impression of power left upon the reader often is very largely

---

* Thackeray.   † Balzac.

that of the creative genius of the author. We wonder how one small head could possibly have contained all the knowledge spun out in chapter after chapter of scenes and incidents involving a multitude of characters. Without this admiration I do not believe a reading public ever would have endured such interminable and tedious productions as Eugène Sue's " Wandering Jew " and Victor Hugo's " Les Miserables." We are amazed at the magnitude of the work, at the intricacy of the plot, at the skilful handling of such a large section of human experience, and, as in the case of the " Wandering Jew," at the range of space involved. We say to ourselves that the author must be a giant in intellect, and we read on and on, spite of our weariness, to find out what new and remarkable circumstance he will give us next. This same interest in the author obtains, as has been remarked, to some extent in every work. His brightness, his cleverness, his constructive power, his faithfulness in reproducing—all influence our feelings; the story first, to be sure, but then, reflectively, the author's genius.

Another form of the impression of power is associated with those effects of the sublime mentioned in the first part of the chapter. I refer to the supernatural, as personality. This is concerned, of course, with the religious sentiments, the basis of which is fear. But this fear gives place to a pleasurable sense of dependence, trust, and faith, whenever we feel that by propitiation we have won the favor of Deity. We thus enter into relations of sympathy with supernatural beings at the same time that we are exalted by their power and majesty. It is the contentment of the child, who feels safe from danger in the protecting care of a parent's greater power. Moreover, fear, though an intrinsically painful emotion, does fix the attention upon the object causing it. Anything, therefore, from which pain is apprehended is necessarily interesting. Fear is not the acute pain of a hurt, but a massive oppression, which first stimulates to find a way of escape from the threatening peril, and then, if none be found, abates all the energies. But in the sympathetic fear which the reader experiences in the narration of dangers menacing the characters of a story, the ultimate effects of the emotion are not felt because, ordinarily, it cannot be made sufficiently strong. The effect of arresting and holding the attention is accomplished, but unless the fear-inspiring situation is held before the mind too long, the reader gets the stimulation without the depression. An exception which proves the rule is, that people of weak nerves, or those who are ill, frequently are unable to bear ghost stories, because the actual terror aroused is so great that they must get rid of it by discontinuing the reading and turning the mind to something else. With the most of people, however, the feeling evoked by

7

such tales is that which is indicated by the phrase "creepy-crawly," which is an emotion of fear strong enough, but not too strong, to fix the attention. Thus, the depiction of power which creates fear is an important element of interest in the story, provided there be not too great intensity or long continuance of the effect.

Such novels as Bulwer's "Zanoni" deal out about the proper modicum of the supernatural, the mysterious, the fear-inspiring; while Poe's stories administer an overdose. In "Zanoni" there is a human and a supernatural interest, and the being through whom the latter is excited is an excellent and admirable character on the whole. The suggestions which stir up fear are relieved by others of a cheerful and enlivening character. Poe, on the other hand, piles horrors upon us without stint or alleviation, until we begin to revert to the author and think him a maniac. He overdoes the matter. It is the fault of most writers who make a specialty of supernatural stories and tales of terror. In Beckford's "Vathek," however, the equilibrium is admirably preserved, but who, nowadays, would admire Walpole's "Castle of Otranto," or Anne Radcliffe's "Mysteries of Udolpho"? Where horror is accumulated without relief, one of two things happens. Either the reader is so painfully shocked that he throws the book down, or the monotony of the terrible disgusts him and he abandons it for that cause.

Allied with this fascination of the supernatural, the fearful, and grewsome is the curiosity excited by mysterious and abnormal natural phenomena. These are available to the novelist for like reasons. There is also, no doubt, a scientific impulse toward inquiry aroused in the reader. The series of tales by Dr. William A. Hammond and the Marquise Clara Lanza, entitled " Tales of Eccentric Life," well illustrate the charm of this kind of fiction; as also does, and most admirably, the more important work of Madame Lanza, " Mr. Perkins's Daughter," wherein the story turns upon the very curious and dramatic circumstance of a "double consciousness " of the heroine.

The use made of the supernatural for ideal creations of the beautiful and the good—angelic and seraphic beings with celestial surroundings—presents power unalloyed by associations of pain and destruction. Hence the popularity of fairy stories. If well constructed, they fulfil very perfectly the conditions of creative art. The difficulty with them is the lack of human interest, which, after all, is necessary to most people for the enjoyment of a work of fiction.

In the general survey now made of the effects of the exhibition of power, we discover that we have reached one generic cause of interest in a romance. It is such because it is an object of engrossing interest in actual experience. Power, as physical force, as mechanism, as skill, as constructive, as destructive, as comprehended or as mysterious, as natural or as supernatural—impresses itself always upon the mind. The course of man's life is one of exertion, of effort, of achievement. Strength means life, growth, development, conservation. In Chapter II. we made a synthesis of pleasures, showing how they all relate to the three functions of growth, preservation, and reproduction. The ends we have been considering in the present chapter are typically the ends of egoistic development and expansion—the enlargement of the individual self. Hence, whatever shows power or strength, whether in exercise or held in reserve, always must be a primary object of sympathetic human interest.

CHAPTER VIII.

THE EXHIBITION OF SUFFERING.

IF one of the chief conditions of æsthetic effect be the rejection or abolition of the disagreeable and painful, the interest felt in the portrayal of suffering would seem to be anomalous; for that such interest exists is undeniable. It proceeds from a variety of sources. We will first consider suffering uncomplicated by moral feelings on the part of the patient, as we find it in sickness, poverty, or misfortune, not associated with guilt or misdemeanor.

Our interest in our fellow human beings proceeds from the gregarious nature of man. An individual cannot attain his own ends of development and perfection, nor gratify his own wants completely, without the use of and aid furnished by others of his own kind. The only way in which he can obtain this assistance at all perfectly is when it is accorded voluntarily. The sole method of creating in another a voluntary disposition to help is to entertain and show a reciprocal willingness to subserve the wishes and ends of that other. Hence, the natural appetite for society, and the birth of sympathy. The interests of a peaceful association of sentient beings cannot be secured without a capacity to enter into the feelings of others, and make them in some degree one's own. The peculiarity of the sympathetic emotions is the attaching of certain feelings relating primarily to ourselves to another personality, and having those feelings aroused by the circumstances of another person or being. These emotions are developed very powerfully through the sexual and family relations. They are also extended to man as man, and even to animals, in the growth of the altruistic character. Selfishness and self-absorbing ends diminish their force.*

There is no novelist who is more successful in the representation of suffering so as to excite sympathy than is Dickens. As M. Taine says :† "There is no writer who knows better how to touch and melt; he makes us weep, absolutely shed tears; before reading him, we did not know there was so much pity in the heart. The grief of a child who wishes to be loved by his father, and whom his father does not love; the despairing love and slow death of a poor, half-imbecile young man—all these pictures of secret grief leave an ineffaceable impression. The tears which he sheds are genuine, and compassion is their only source."

---

* "System of Psychology," Part VI., ch. xlv.
† "English Literature," Book V., ch. i.

Probably his most characteristic portrayals are those of the miseries of children in ill conditions. We at once think of Little Nell, Little Jo, and David Copperfield as types of this class of sufferers. It is easy to see in such cases that the parental feelings are the foundation of the pity and sorrow we feel at the hard and distressful fate of these characters. This grief we should not experience, were it not that the author first creates a very lovable personality, in whom our interest increases, and with whom we are more and more disposed to sympathize. A volume of tender emotion is generated, which is in itself agreeable. This produces a greater sensitiveness to events which supposably affect painfully the person toward whom the tender feelings flow. But when such incidents occur, it is a mistake to suppose that the sympathetic emotions springing up are unadulterated pain. On the contrary, they are largely pleasurable. There is the tender feeling, admiration for the character, the skilful weaving of the plot, the beauty of description, the rising desire to relieve the suffering. Even when we are moved to tears, their flow is a relief and an assuagement, succeeded by a calm and the pleasure of repose.

In contemplating the approach of death there are other emotions. We are in the presence of the great Mystery of Power. The sublime, the supernatural overshadow us, and with our human sympathies go along an awe at the power which controls life and transcends knowledge, and also a yearning faith that prompts us to lift up

> " A voice as unto Him that hears,
> A cry above the conquered years,
> To one that with us works."

The religious aspirations, sympathies, and joys are aroused in the solemn passing of one whom we have learned to love. Sorrow there is, but there is also peace and hope, and often trust. Deep feeling, indeed, fills us when we read the following passage from " The Old Curiosity Shop," but that feeling is not pain. We do not seek to rid ourselves of it ; we rather cherish it. " They saw the vault covered and the stone fixed down. Then, when the dusk of evening had come on, and not a sound disturbed the sacred stillness of the place, when the bright moon poured in her light on tomb and monument, on pillar, wall, and arch, and most of all (it seemed to them) upon her quiet grave—in that calm time, when outward things and inward thoughts teem with assurances of immortality, and worldly hopes and fears are humbled in the dust before them—then, with tranquil and submissive hearts they turned away, and left the child with God.

" Oh ! it is hard to take to heart the lesson that such deaths will teach ; but let no man reject it, for it is one all must learn, and is a mighty, uni-

versal truth. When death strikes down the innocent and young, for every fragile form from
which he lets the panting spirit free a hundred
virtues rise, in shapes of mercy, charity, and love,
to walk the world and bless it. Of every tear
that sorrowing mortals shed on such green graves
some good is born, some gentler nature comes.
In the destroyer's steps there spring up bright
creations that defy his power, and his dark path
becomes a way of light to heaven."

In reading the description of the sickness and
death of "Ivan Ilyitch," by Tolstoï, the sources
of our interest are somewhat different. We do not
care much for Ivan, still less for his family, or anybody else introduced into the story. We have no
tenderness such as we feel for Little Nell or Little
Jo. Nor is there anything beautiful connected
with Ivan's life, nor any compensating thought or
imagination suggested by his death. We are held
by a scientific interest in the development of the
man's disease and his own attitude toward it.
We follow Ivan's analyses and speculations, we
occupy ourselves with his symptoms, his depres-
sions, his frights, his despair. It is a medical, a
pathological interest. But this is not all. We are
fascinated by the horror of the situation. We
cannot get away if we try. I have no doubt this
is the explanation of a great deal of the attraction
horrors have in novels. It is the force of the
"*idée fixe*," which paralyzes and chains. When,

in the course of our lives, we see a horrible accident which we are unable to prevent, we are pow-
erless to take our eyes off, though the vision be
exceedingly distressing. If a human being be
caught in a machine-belt before us, or be dashed
from a carriage on a pile of rock, we are spell-
bound and are forced to witness the course of
events to their end, because unable to withdraw
our gaze. In all this there is no element of pleasure, nor can there be in the representation of such
things in a story, excepting always in the reflection upon the author's genius as a word-painter.
But descriptions of this sort will enthrall the
reader for a time. If, however, they are too long-
continued, he will throw off his paralysis and refuse to submit himself longer to the influencing
cause. The effect is, in itself, not æsthetic. Its
value in literature, apart from the bearings of the
incident on the plot, is that its production is a
very good device for holding the attention.
Where the horrible occurrences are made the entire plot of the story, the only permanent interest
is, as in "Ivan Ilyitch," the value of the narration
as a physiological and·psychological study.

Let us now turn to those cases of suffering, the
burden of which is some error, wrong, or crime
entailing direful consequences. In this category,
we may notice first, sins growing out of the relations of the sexes, such as form the principal subject of Scott's "Heart of Midlothian," George

Eliot's "Adam Bede," Hawthorne's "Scarlet Letter," and Tolstoï's "Anna Karénina." In the first
two of these, crime in the form of infanticide occurs, and the whole course of misfortune falling
upon a woman from irregular relations with a man
is set forth, forming the main interest. Yet there
are a good many subsidiary interests in both these
books. In the one the descriptions of English
country life, and in the other of Scotch peasantry,
are of themselves exceedingly entertaining, and
no doubt would have made the books popular
with an entirely different plot. Possessing this
background of interest, the misfortunes of the
two principal characters arouse sympathy, the
pleasurable quality of which is greatly enhanced
by the fact that, after undergoing grave peril, they
get out of their difficulties. The excitement of
danger always adds to the glow of satisfaction
when the relief comes. In addition, there is a
very strong moral force in the incidents, which is
often a source of great satisfaction to the reader.
He sympathizes with Effie and Hetty, but the
sympathy is somewhat of the parent with the
child upon whom he has inflicted punishment.
He is sorry for the delinquent, to be sure, but on
the whole rather glad to have him punished. But
the reader's sympathetic pain cannot, in the nature
of things, be as strong as that of the loving parent
for the whipped child. The reader, too, thinks
of the general moral and educational effect, and

while he is glad that the young women escaped death, he is pleased on the score of justice, morality, and religion that they were taught a severe lesson. Those of a less stern nature, who would entertain the retributory sentiments to a less degree and whose sympathies are stronger for the woes of the wrong-doers, will feel that exaltation of the emotional nature which tender feeling always causes, and also will have in their own way a moral joy, believing that,

" The noblest pity on the earth
Is that bestowed on sin." *

Another reflection should occur to us with reference to all accounts of weakness, suffering, and crime. The incidents of suffering and the characters undergoing it serve as a foil to set off stronger characters and give them an opportunity to display the noble qualities of human nature:

" The gods in bounty work up storms about us,
That give mankind occasion to exert
Their hidden strength, and throw out into practice
Virtues which shun the day and lie concealed
In the smooth seasons and the calms of life." †

Mountains would not be grand were it not for plains and valleys; strong men would not be strong were none weak; goodness would not shine were there no evil; and against the ill-for-

---

* J. G. Holland.   † Addison.

tunes of Effie Deans and Hetty we have a proper
and satisfactory compensation in the characters
of Jeanie Deans in the one story, and Adam Bede
and Dinah in the other.

The "Scarlet Letter" and "Anna Karénina"
present some points of similarity with respect to
the present topic. It is no part of the purpose of
this essay to pass judgment on any book cited,
nor to estimate, either absolutely or comparatively,
its merits as a literary product, beyond what is
necessary for the purposes of illustration. Readers
will doubtless miss some of their favorites and
very likely be able to suggest better illustrations
than those I employ. This is inevitable, on account of differences in taste and the vast amount
of material to select from. All that is aimed at
here is to choose fairly representative examples.
In this view I bring together the works just mentioned. Setting aside the differences in style, in
incident, in scene, in nationality, there is a community between the two in that both are an exhibition of the slow course of retributory suffering
to a woman from irregular indulgence. The contrast between them is in the final result, which in
the case of Anna Karénina is unbalanced mind
and horrible suicide, but in Hester Prynne is a
new life chastened and beatified, a source of com-
fort and help to others. The one is the cruci-
fixion without the resurrection, the other with it.
In both of these books the interest is primarily

moral.   E. M. de Vogüé speaks of " Anna Karénina " as a " manual of morals " in Russia, yet
there is no question but, viewing the two from this
ground, the " Scarlet Letter " leaves a much better
impression, inasmuch as hope is brought to the
foreground instead of despair.   This is the com-
pensatory relief of which I have spoken, for which
the reader has a conscious or unconscious longing.
In the Russian novel it is found, so far as it goes,
in the change of heart of Levin, and his contented
life.   It must be said, however, that this did not
help Anna Karénina very much.   The influence of
Tolstoï's book, then, may be educationally good;
its issue, so far as relates to the Karénins, may satisfy the sense of justice; but the merciful element,
which appears in the " Scarlet Letter," is wanting.

In realistic description of suffering the interest may be held on the principle of the *idée fixe*,
which we considered in a recent paragraph.   Victor Hugo's " Le Dernier Jour d'un Condemné " illustrates this sort of writing; and more strikingly
still, Dostoyevsky's " Crime and Punishment."
The remorse and fear of Jonas in " Martin Chuz-
zlewit " may also be cited among several good examples from Dickens.   " Crime and Punishment,"
though perhaps not so generally known as the
others, furnishes certainly one of the very strong-
est exhibitions in literature of the subjective
effects of crime upon the criminal, the workings
of fear and remorse upon an impressionable

nature, at last making life intolerable and bringing the sufferer to the verge of madness. But in every successful book containing the portrayal of this sort of experience there is always something to relieve the tension of the reader's mind and redeem the horror of the situation ; and those just cited form no exception. The pictures of Russian life in " Crime and Punishment " are entertaining, and the final eventual liberation of the sufferer and his spiritual redemption through the devotion of the girl Sonia, who also is rescued from degradation, bring the story to an agreeable conclusion. As for Dickens, every one knows how he alternates tears and laughter, and never permits to the reader a monotony of feeling.

Inasmuch as we shall in a subsequent chapter refer to the novels of "manners," exhibiting social movements and conditions, we will not at present dwell upon narratives of general social wretchedness, such as have been produced by Dickens, Eugène Sue, Victor Hugo, Balzac, M. Zola, and the Russians. They do not display any sources of interest other than those already mentioned, save that of social progress and development. But something more may be said with reference to stories of war and battle scenes which present suffering in its most terrible form. In these I think there is often that predatory joy of killing which was spoken of in the last chapter. This surely is an element of the interest in stories of the hunting down of criminals or the destruction of robbers and pirates in combat. The moral sense of justice reconciles us to our wolfish pleasure and makes us believe that our lack of sympathy or our positive antipathy is very praiseworthy. Nevertheless, disguise it as we may, there is a subtle, malignant, and devilish pleasure in seeing people hunted, tortured, and killed. If there be revenge, it adds wonderfully to this delight. Whether we read the detective stories of Gaboriau, the brutal scenes of the Smollett tribe of novelists, or the realistic descriptions of "Sebastopol" and "War and Peace," * we are more or less animated by the ecstasy that makes the Indian preparing for war dance around the fire with uplifted tomahawk and think voluptuously of the scalps of the morrow. The more brutal the nature the more this lust is stimulated. To be sure there are comparatively few readers who are not controlled by other and better sentiments ; but the desire for vengeance we have always with us in some degree ; and, quite independently of this, there are always some eager to give the *pollice verso* sign. Indeed, more of us than would admit it are glad to have an infusion of the blood-fury in the stories that occupy our leisure. We like to see the devil "skelp" and "scaud" poor wretches and hear them squeal. We admire the exhibition

---

* Tolstoï.

of the power of Ulysses in his fight with Irus, but we also enjoy seeing the beggar smashed.

Further than this, all the pleasures of witnessing the display of strength and skill leading to success which we mentioned fully in the last chapter form the main interests in war scenes, with the moral feelings aroused by suffering and its tender suggestions as variations. The heroic generally causes us to forget the brutal. Where the latter is brought before us, however, we are interested either from the fascination of the *idée fixe*, or from latent fierceness and cruelty and the spirit of revenge in our own sentiments. It is fortunately the case that on the whole the sympathetic side of human nature is growing more controlling and we demand more and more that our sympathies be ministered unto. Then it is endurance, self-sacrifice, devotion to a cause, courage in the face of attack rather than in attacking, that command our greatest interest, inasmuch as we feel with Carlyle that " the essential function of the soldier is not killing but being killed."

To sum up : the exhibition of suffering interests us sympathetically, from developing pleasurable tender emotion, finding its issue in pity, sorrow, tears ; morally, from its bearings on moral character, on justice, education, and human welfare generally ; scientifically, from its psychological and pathological phenomena ; brutally, from the enjoyment we share with other carnivorous ani-

8

mals in pursuing, tearing, and killing prey ; and, once more, from the serpent fascination of the *idée fixe*, which holds us to the contemplation of horrors against our will.*

---

*The *Forum* for September, 1889, contains an excellent article by Mr. James Sully, whose title, ' The Luxury of Pity," explains sufficiently its relation to the present topic.

CHAPTER IX.

THE EXHIBITION OF LOVE.

THAT accomplished scholar and critic, Mr. Brander Matthews, in an essay entitled " The Philosophy of the Short-story," * explains that one great difference between the short-story and the novel proper " lies in the fact that the novel, nowadays at least, must be a love-tale, while the short-story need not deal with love at all." " Since love is almost the only thing which will give interest to a long story, the writer of novels has to get love into his tales as best he may, even when the subject rebels and when he himself is too old to take any interest in the mating of John and Joan. But the short-story, being brief, does not need a love-interest to hold its parts together, and the writer of short-stories has thus a greater free- · dom ; he may do as he pleases ; from him a love-tale is not expected."

No doubt Mr. Matthews is correct in his statement of what has been and is the inexorability of the demand for a love-interest of some sort in

---

* " Pen and Ink."

every novel.   So far has this gone that its existence
seems, in the minds of some, to be the distinctive
character of prose fiction.   For instance, we run
across this very extraordinary definition by P.
Bayne: " The novel is a domestic history, whose
whole interest centres in a tale of love." I wonder what this oracle would call Mr. Stevenson's
" Jekyll and Hyde " !   I suppose he would reckon
it as a short-story, though Mr. Matthews does not
think the work compressed enough to be fairly so
called.   But a story it is ; it is highly interesting,
and there is no domestic history involving love.
If it had been a little longer, we could still have
got along without love ; but if it had been ex-
panded to three volumes, the amatory interest
being still absent, probably we should have missed
something.   The reason of this is, as seems to me,
not that love is indispensable to interest, which is
surely not the case, but rather that we cannot produce a correct representation of any considerable
portion of human experience without encounter-
ing the influences and effects of this passion.
Dealing with half a dozen, a dozen, a score of
characters, male and female, if we cover very
much of their careers and take account of no manifestation of love—romantic, conjugal, or parental
—our edifice is lop-sided, imperfectly and unnat-
urally constructed.   Love plays so prominent a
part in life, has so dominant an influence on conduct, that its absence as a motive is at once felt

by the reader, and the plot from which it is omitted seems very artificial.

The topic of suffering has served as a bridge to conduct us naturally from one extreme form of human interest to another. The pleasures and ends which were indicated in our treatment of the Exhibition of Power are, as we noted at the close of Chapter VII., those of individual egoistic development. They are characteristically the selfish interests. In the last chapter we saw how the entrance of sympathetic emotion tended to soften the selfishness of human nature and create a genuine altruistic sentiment. We now pass to a powerful altruistic interest : the individual, through the appetites of society and sex, coming to find his happiness in that of others in forming ends of life, and seeking satisfaction of them in reproduction or race development. Since he, the individual, must die, he will endeavor to perpetuate himself in his offspring. This he does instinctively, and the appetites and passions leading to this result are often stronger than the motives to self-preservation.

These facts of human constitution furnish ample explanation of the interest which the exhibition of love in its various forms creates in the reader of a novel. Love between the sexes in itself, the love of husband and wife, and parental affection, are the three chief modes in which the sentiment is made to appear; and of these the first and third·

furnish the best situations for the development of incident.   Movement interests rather than rest, becoming rather than being.   Our attention is more readily held by the process of uniting or disuniting, the pursuit of an end sought, than by a calm monotony of life, wherein nothing in particular occurs.   No doubt much happier are they who have no history; but the reader of their chronicles will be better satisfied if the river of life flows less smoothly.

Love, as we employ the term in this chapter, exhibits the workings of two natural, primary, fundamental appetites: society and sex.   The former was described sufficiently in the last chapter as the innate desire for the amicable presence of others of one's kind.   If we trace this want to its ultimate sources, I think we should find it in the pleasure of soft, warm contact, which induces cows to rub against each other and squirrels to nestle together.   It causes a transmission of vitality.   If to this primitive sensibility we add the sexual promptings, we have the foundation for the establishment of gregariousness.   These two elements are developed in varying relations with respect to each other.   The society-appetite favors unselfishness, because, as we saw, there is no society without reciprocity.   The sex-appetite is much more egoistic.   But even to its gratification a reciprocal interest becomes important, and when there is superadded parental love we often have

exemplified the most utter self-abnegation. The
sex-appetite is more intense and imperious than
the other, but it is also more evanescent. It often
goes out in smoke—unless the flame be fed with
the fuel which the appetite for society supplies.
The social wants extend over the whole of life
and favor the formation of remote ends and purposes, toward which the efforts of a career may
converge. The sex impulses are concentrated and
. limited. They are more emotional and passional,
less intellectual and representative. They are
fiercer and less manageable. The others are more
sustained and more readily controlled.

There is in love between the sexes always a
combination of the social and the purely sexual;
the former issuing in the higher and more spiritual developments of the sentiment, the latter in
lower appetitive satisfactions. In narrative exhibitions of this passion it is possible, therefore, to
present both sides, but there are many reasons
why the manifestations of the sex-appetite are
generally not deemed fit subjects for the novelist's
portrayals. With regard to social interests, there
is a wide range from those sentiments which make
of love a projected life-interest, involving marriage, children, and all the kinds of community
which a unity of life involves, to its spontaneous
breaking forth as an emotion sufficient for itself
in the present, without regard for its future
advantages and utilities. The latter exempli-

fies love in its complete development as a passion.

Of course, the reader's interest is a sympathetic one; and, so far as the incidents call for it, there exists the sympathy with suffering of which we spoke in the last chapter. Many of the stories of blighted affection, of harassing obstacles to the fruition of love, of married unhappiness, upon which George Sand is so fond of dwelling, or such as we find in " Middlemarch " * or in " Daniele · Cortice," † illustrate these conditions. But the characteristic interest is rather that which we have in a strong motive force, governing action and possessing the whole nature. In the words of Balzac: ‡ " We may here remark on the infiltrating, transforming power of an overmastering emotion. However coarse the fibre of the individual, let him be held by a strong and genuine affection, and he exhales, as it were, an essence, which illuminates his features, inspires his gestures, and gives cadence to his voice. It happens sometimes that the dullest soul, under the lash of passion, attains to such eloquence of thought, if not of language, that it seems to move in luminous air." Love, therefore, is really, after all said, an exhibition of power, but of introsusceptive, assimilative, constructive power, of transfiguration and transformation; not the triumph of

---

* George Eliot.   † Foggazaro.   ‡ " Père Goriot."

muscular energy nor the putting forth of brute force.

Any of the great passions of human life which seize hold of and possess men—like anger, revenge, avarice, lust, ambition—interest the reader when effectively set forth by the novelist. Many story-writers have made their reputation, as Bayne says of Charlotte Brontë, "by the delineation of one relentless and tyrannizing passion." The causes of this interest have been already explained. But the generally benevolent and beneficent character of love creates a superior interest in those who are sufficiently cultivated to belong to the recognized reading public. True, the popularity of cheap tales of blood and adventure, of "shilling thrillers," admonishes us not to believe that the educated and refined are the only readers of stories. With the vulgarized and brutalized, a good love-story is either something obscene or it is some wild romance of abduction and pursuit, of jealousy and murder because of women. But people of this order do not write criticisms on books, nor do they give the tone to critical comments. Our estimate, then, of the excellence of a love-romance is based upon the fact that it appeals to the more refined, the amiable, the kindly, the loving. It is, hence, perfectly correct to say that the interest in love is greater than in any other absorbing passion, because of its more humane character.

Love is more æsthetic, since its painful associations are fewer. To be sure, the course of true love may not run smooth, but in the emotion itself or its satisfaction there is involved no suggestion of pain. If Ajax be a magnificent warrior, he becomes such only by killing somebody, and we must sometimes think of ·the men killed. If Herbert Hollister and Stuart Goldwin, in an "Ambitious Woman," * win their hundreds of thousands in Wall Street, and command our admiration for their sagacity, their intuitive and unerring judgment, we know that somebody lost ; and, indeed, the meaning of that loss shortly appears, with all its horrors, in the case of the first-named. On the other hand, in the union of two personalities effected by love there is, intrinsically and essentially, nothing but agreeable suggestion, whether it be the "mating of John and Joan," or of a lord and lady. It really is the flowering of human experience, the acme of the joyful, the delightful, the blissful, the beautiful. Pain is banished, and there is only the breath of the spring, "fresh-blown roses washed in dew," "youthful jollity," "wreathed smiles," and

"Sport, that wrinkled Care derides." †

Of love we think

---

* Edgar Fawcett.   † Milton : "L'Allegro."

" As of a fountain, failing never,
   On whose soft marge I lie, and drink
   Delicious draughts of joy forever." *

Thus, of the great passions, love is undoubtedly
the richest in æsthetic qualities. While science
cannot at present make this assertion, I deem it
probable that all the æsthetic effects which we
receive through the senses, whether they be the
delights of music or of color, perception by the
eye generally or by the ear, involve a stimulation
of amatory feeling. This is not the place to go
into a psychological argument on the subject, but
the reader who is familiar with Darwin's " Descent
of Man " may be reminded of the facts therein
collected going to prove that bright and diversi-
fied colors and also musical sounds are means of
sexual attraction. Moreover, the connection of
æsthetic activity with the play-impulse has already
occupied our attention. But play occurs from a
superabundance of vitality; when the spirits are
high, and there is more vital force than is needed
for self-preservation. And it is in just this condition that reproductive activity, mental or physical,
is the most pronounced. It is the excess beyond
what is required for the preservation and development of the individual organism. Moreover, the
exercise of this activity is always an end in itself,
a primary appetitive pleasure. It needs no object

* Owen Meredith.

beyond its own satisfaction. May it not be possible, therefore, that we shall discover our productive, creative, artistic working to be really a
manifestation of the forces of organic reproduction, and our æsthetic joy in its works the re-
sponse made to an appeal addressed to the same
vital powers ?

However this may be, it is quite certain that
the superior interest felt in the exhibition of love
both in life and in literature is the æsthetic one.
But this interest is of the different varieties before
mentioned. The greatest intensity arises from
consideration of the passion as such, irrespective
of its consequences. In this the French writers
vastly surpass any others, and in this English
novelists are singularly lacking. Such might be
expected from national characteristics. So far as
the former are concerned, in the words of Mr. W.
C. Brownell : * "Certainly more distinctly and
universally than anywhere else is it felt in France
that love *vincit omnia*—that it is, as Thackeray af-
firms, 'immeasurably above ambition, more pre-
cious than wealth, more noble than name,' and that
'he knows not life who knows not that.'" The
French value most of all, and for its own sake,
"the spiritual exaltation of the least egoistic of
human impulses. Never to have made the voy-
age to Cythera is to have lived in vain." †   Thus,

---

* " French Traits " : Morality.   † (Ibid.)

devoted to a passion, they develop its intensity and seek all its refinements, whereas the colder and calmer natures of the English think more of the duration of the sentiment, its association and blending with other forms of tender emotion and with altruistic sympathies generally. It thus happens with leading English-writing novelists, as Henry James remarks : * " Miss Austen and Sir Walter Scott, Dickens and Thackeray, Hawthorne and George Eliot, have all represented young people in love with each other ; but no one of them has, to the best of our recollection, described anything that can be called a passion—put it into motion before us and shown us its various paces." Then referring to George Sand, a critique upon whom elicits these observations, Mr. James goes on to say : " Few persons would resort to English prose fiction for any information concerning the ardent forces of the heart, for any ideas upon them. It is George Sand's merit that she has given ideas upon them, that she has enlarged the novel-reader's conception of them and proved herself in all that relates to them an authority. This is a great deal. From this standpoint Miss Austen, Walter Scott, and Dickens will appear to have omitted the erotic sentiment altogether, and George Eliot will seem to have treated it with singular austerity. Strangely loveless, seen in this

---

* " French Poets and Novelists " : George Sand.

light, are those large, comprehensive fictions, ' Middlemarch ' and ' Daniel Deronda.' They seem
to foreign readers, probably, like vast, cold, com-
modious, respectable rooms, through whose win-
dow-panes one sees a snow-covered landscape, and
across whose acres of silver-lined carpet one looks
in vain for a fire-place or a fire."

Quite so. The English and Americans are in-
capable, it would seem, of dealing with love as a
passion. They insist on the moral complexion.
As M. Taine suggests,* they always say : " Be
moral. . . . Love is the hero of all George
Sand's novels. Married or not, she thinks it
beautiful, holy, sublime in itself ; and she says so.
Don't believe this, and if you believe it, don't say
it. It is a bad example. Love thus represented
makes marriage a secondary matter. . . . A
novel of this sort is a plea for the heart, the imagination, enthusiasm, nature ; but it is also often a
plea against society and law ; we do not suffer
society and law to be touched, directly or indirectly. . . . George Sand paints impassioned
women ; paint you for us good women. George
Sand makes us desire to be in love ; do you make
us desire to be married." Now, dear friends, English and American, M. Taine is quite right. You
may argue that your views and your course should
be approved. Perhaps ; but on moral grounds.

---

* ' Hist. of Eng. Lit.," Book V., ch. i.

Follow your own convictions, if you please, but do not pretend to any equality with George Sand, for example, in the sphere which she occupies. Say frankly that your stories are more moral and less freely artistic ; that they do not exhibit love in any fulness, but only as subsidiary to marriage and moral and social interests. Then when comparisons are made, your work on the whole may be deemed the more wholesome, but as an exhibition of a great passion it is painfully insufficient. You cannot compete ; and it will be wiser to say so, seeking for your justification where you ought, in the subordination of the æsthetic to the moral for the sake of human welfare.

But in representations of that calmer love of wedded life, which is really a close and increasing friendship cemented by many common interests, and in depicting characters in which love is always controlled by morality and duty, English and American novelists are greatly superior to their Gallic brethren. If the French have no word in their language for home, it is quite true that they have little room for home or domesticity in their novels. It would not be fair to say that this is because they do not value the domestic life and the maintenance of happy families. It is rather because the regular and normal development of love and marriage or marriage and wedded love does not afford material for dramatic effect and is too monotonous to arouse interest in minds which desire excitement and novelty. Anglo-Saxon natures are different. They are satisfied with what would seem tame to a Frenchman. An ordinary domestic history is interesting to them, inasmuch as, in the first place, they do not require so much stimulation, and again, and perhaps chiefly, because they think an account of the " happy family " has an excellent moral and educational effect. Hence they are pleased with Maria Edgeworth's tales and with E. P. Roe's novels. The chief interest is an ethical one; and if monotony is to be avoided, they prefer to introduce the successful struggles of a virtuous soul against temptation, to show forth the persistence of fidelity, the claims of honor and of duty under trying circumstances, the chastening influence of suffering, and the triumph of the moral principles of human nature. All these things are interesting to readers whose minds are so constituted that they can readily sympathize with the events and characters of the narration from the domination in themselves of the domestic affections and the moral sentiments in general.

Intrinsically, the perils incurred and the sufferings experienced by an intrepid heroine who is determined to follow the promptings of illicit love are just as interesting as the struggle of another to adhere to the path of rectitude against the demands of overpowering passion, and her success, though with much tribulation and unhappiness; but in the latter case the sentiment of moral approval will greatly heighten the effect of the story, in precisely the same way as in actual life we take greater pleasure in a person who has exhibited in the face of obstacles and diversions a degree of moral stamina which has made what we esteem virtue to become ascendent in his mind and in his deeds.

The sources of interest in the exhibition of love in a story are thus evident, whether we behold the force and movements of the passion or the various associations and resultants as seen in the development of family and home life. It remains for us to say a word respecting the nature of the interest aroused by minute and extreme descriptions of the course of erotic appetite. We cannot disguise from ourselves the fact that such interest is chiefly a fascination which involves the excitation of sexual appetite. But one thing must not be lost sight of. The erotic passion is not constant and universal throughout human life, and where it is wanting, there is frequently disgust at its suggestion. In fact, it may be said that the large majority of people over forty would derive no satisfaction from reading distinctively erotic literature. It is tedious and offensive. The witnessing of amatory familiarities in real life is not agreeable, nor is their representation in a story. On the contrary, it is esteemed indecent and even filthy, though to a person in the hey-day of youth the idea of uncleanliness in such associations may be absolutely wanting and itself indecent. From these facts arises that singular contradiction of tastes, by which we find erotic stories of absorbing interest to some and pleasing to their minds, while hateful to others and unsparingly condemned by them. At all events, it is evident that such tales or such episodes cannot be universally interesting, quite apart from moral considerations. They must appeal to a limited class of readers, with the risk of great antipathy from those who do not enjoy reading them.

CHAPTER X.

THE three chapters last preceding make clear to us that the objects of interest in a story are simply the objects of interest in human life itself. The developments of individual character in action, the putting forth of strength positively or in resistance, the movement of vitality in achievement, power in some form or other—these are the things that detain our attention, whether in the real world or that of fiction. But no man is great in isolation. Whatever he accomplishes, bears relation to his fellows. In considering him, we also consider his environment, and whatever interest we take in his career requires an interest in his surroundings. This involves some account of the general social movement ; of the ideas, the conditions, the habits that dominate the social world. The novelist cannot avoid making a "*milieu*," an "*entourage*" for his characters, and it often occurs that the characters themselves are made secondary to and illustrative of particular social conditions, which it is the author's chief aim to exhibit.

The decline of romantic and heroic literature is very obvious. For it has been substituted, in prose fiction, by novels dealing with ordinary social life, with " manners," with analysis of character, and with the study of motives. The reason for this change is the increasing predominance of the industrial spirit over the militant in governing human life in general. There is no longer a career for the mailed knight who goes forth with his sword and lance in search of adventures. His courage and heroism would only land him in the penitentiary. The ideals which people form of things possible to be done are those conditioned by a peaceful industrial civilization, in which skill supersedes brute force, and virtue is rectitude rather than the soldier's valor. The objects which interest the mind are determined accordingly, and the novel-reader demands something akin to his own occupations and agreeable to his prevailing sympathies. He wants to see portrayed the people of his own day and generation, with whom he is at home, and who suggest something to his mind. By such only is he aroused, edified, or improved. Among these is tragedy enough and comedy enough, virtue and vice sufficient for all requirements. They are real to him ; he can understand them, and they assimilate with his own thought and feeling. They are more serviceable for all purposes which make the novel of value.

It may be doubted whether studies of society

as it is afford in themselves any better opportunities for æsthetic construction than do romances, so called. A fairy-tale may be deliciously
beautiful—perfect as a work of art. Fouqué's
" Undine " is a most charming production. Hans
Christian Andersen's stories are thoroughly artistic. When we consider that the world of imagination is the realm of creative art, which is, after all,
the highest; and that poetry, which is full of imaginative creations, is addressed to the æsthetic
sense most conspicuously of all forms of literature
—we shall see that the romance may be a work of
very high artistic quality. But still there is the
fact upon which we commented in discussing realism in Chapter VI. One sign of a great artist is
his ability to glorify the commonplace and make
us see beauty in ordinary things. A genius cannot
paint a tree without revealing himself, and if we
have the eye to see we shall recognize him, and
be delighted with him. A sheep is not a particularly interesting animal ; but if Verböckhoven has
painted one, we stop and look at the picture. So
the novelist may present scenes of familiar life
with such consummate skill that we cannot prevent the holding of our attention, even when we
do not expect to be entertained. Turgénieff is
a writer who characteristically does this. " He
makes realism poetic."*   What is there especially

* E. M. de Vogüé.

uncommon about a man, whose unfaithful wife
is separated from him, falling in love with a young
girl in whose family he is a frequent visitor?
Nor does it require much ingenuity for the author
to supply a false report of the death of the wife,
and then, after the lovers had declared themselves,
bring the wife back to shatter their hopes and
blight their lives. This is the story of " Liza,"
which in the hands of some writers would be dull
and stupid, but as told by the great Russian, is
finished, compact, consistent, vivid, attractive, and
thoroughly interesting. It is such artistic power
that gives popularity to the works of writers like
Mr. Howells, of whom Col. T. W. Higginson says :
" His first literary principle has been to look away
from great passions, and rather to elevate the commonplace by minute touches." *   So it is said of
George Eliot that " she made ordinary people
interesting." †   Indeed, the ability to do these
things has been urgently claimed as one of the
great artistic merits of the realistic method. This
is the view of Mr. George Parsons Lathrop, in a
magazine article : ‡   " Realism sets itself at work
to consider characters and events which are apparently the most ordinary and uninteresting in order
to extract from these their full value and meaning. It would apprehend in all particulars the

---

* " Short Studies."   † Bayard Tuckerman.
          ‡ *Atlantic Monthly*, 1874.

connection between the familiar and the extraordinary, and the seen and the unseen of human
nature. Beneath the deceptive cloak of outwardly
uneventful days it detects and endeavors to trace
the outlines of the spirits that are hidden there;
to measure the changes in their growth, to watch
the symptoms of moral decay or regeneration; to
fathom their histories of passionate or intellectual
problems. In short, realism reveals. Where we
thought nothing worthy of notice, it shows everything to be rife with significance."

I should certainly decline to award to " realism "
the sole credit for " revealing " in the sense of the
word just employed. As I have endeavored to
show, the unrestricted and unqualified use of the
naturalistic method dulls that æsthetic perception
which is necessary for arriving at the soul of things.
Something more is needed. Mr. Lathrop really
concedes this, for immediately after the above
passage he makes the important statement : " It
will easily be seen, therefore, that realism calls
upon imagination to exercise its highest function."
When realism does this, it is a good thing; but its
tendencies are not always that way. There is no
use, however, in quarrelling about words. It is
certain, at all events, that one of the very highest
achievements of art is to invest the apparently
uninteresting with an interest which to our minds
makes it cease to be commonplace, and stand out
with a distinctness and individuality that give it

a permanent life. And however necessary to the result anatomical study may be, close inspection of nature as she is, actually and ordinarily,·it is creative genius that finally accomplishes the work.

With the progress of the industrial spirit the scientific mind has become more developed and scientific methods are in greater demand for everything. Sociological and psychological analyses excite attention, as they would not if scientific observation were not a common habit. Thus, novels of "experiment," as M. Zola calls them, are read and become popular, whereas under the conditions of life when romanticism was in vogue they would not have been endured. The latter, as Mr. Howells observes, "was the expression of a world mood." "It grew naturally out of political, social, and economical conditions." "It was a development of civilization." In like manner, the present age has produced literature after its own kind. Knowledge of things as they are is demanded, and thorough knowledge. With the increase of learning and the higher training of individuals to use their own faculties, people demand also that better artistic work be done, and when they see such work they know it.

In fine, the prevalence and success of the novels of social life furnish but another illustration of the truth that it is life which makes literature, and that the type of fiction of any age is determined by the state of thought and civilization therein.

But we must not forget that what De Quincey calls the "literature of power" is that which makes its appeal to universal human experience, and that if "the representation of social reality" be at present "the proper business of the novel," it is still important, as D. Masson says, that in such representation the spirit be "that of the far-surveying and the sublime."

CHAPTER XI.

THE COMIC OR LUDICROUS.

OUR study thus far has indicated that in order to hold the attention upon a work of fiction some sort of sympathetic interest must be aroused, or else a paralyzing effect be produced which inhibits escape. This last situation cannot endure very long, because a narration appealing to the imagination can rarely excite unpleasant emotions powerful enough to prevent the natural movements to get rid of the object producing them, and because an accumulation of horrors tends to monotony, which is itself detrimental to interest. Even where there is sympathy aroused, no little difficulty is experienced from the danger of monotony. We have remarked how skilful writers do not play long upon one emotional chord, but attain their best effects by exciting a variety of feelings. Where the attention is concentrated sufficiently to create interest a considerable quantity of emotion exists, the fulness of which will cause uneasiness or positive pain. This must be disposed of in some way.

Transferring the attention to some object

strongly contrasted with the former one will accomplish this result in many cases; in order, however, to effect the transfer, the new object must possess the power of concentrating a considerable amount of feeling upon itself. But merely changing the object while still exciting and massing feeling will not furnish the relief needed. The very process of changing becomes monotonous and tiresome. A complete dissipation of aroused and concentrated emotion is required, a full relaxation from the strain of attention. This is most perfectly secured by laughter in its various degrees.

There is much yet to be explained in the phenomenon of laughter. Sydney Smith says that mirth is due to the discovery of a congruity in a seeming incongruity, or the reverse. The seeing of a joke is analogous to the pleasant mental feeling experienced in discovering something quite new, or in suddenly coming to understand something not known before. But in case of the joke the discovery comes as a surprise, something achieved without toil, and the pleasurable effect is thereby much heightened. In relation to the need of a wooden pavement before St. Paul's, Sydney Smith remarked: " If the Dean and the Chapter would only lay their heads together the thing would be done." Here the " laugh comes in " when the mind perceives a congruity in the midst of extremely incongruous things. It makes

no difference whether the implication of wooden-
headedness, or stupidity, as against the Dean and
the Chapter, be true or not.   The striking out of
a resemblance unexpectedly is quite enough to
secure the effect of mirth.

This example illustrates the existence of another element in the production of mirth, which is
pointed out by Dr. Bain, and consists in the degradation of some person or thing ordinarily possessing dignity.   The same idea is contained in
Hobbes's theory that "laughter is a sudden glory
arising from sudden conception of some eminency
in ourselves by comparison with the infirmity of
others, or with our own formerly."   In the example last cited laughter arises from the exposure of
the inferiority of those who are ordinarily held in
solemn reverence.   We enjoy having them "taken
down a peg."   Mr. Herbert Spencer asserts that
the incongruity perceived in the ludicrous is always a descending, never an ascending, incongruity.

"What should be great you turn to farce." *
Mr. Spencer, however, does not lay stress on the
fact of exultation over degradation so much as on
the circumstance of passing from something great
to something small.   It would seem, though, that
the state of mind described by Hobbes, and more
particularly by Dr. Bain, is generally found pres-

* Prior.

ent when we are moved to laughter. In the savage mind laughter is the exultation of victory or revenge. The warrior's joy over the discomfited foe is his mirth. So, more civilized men of coarse instincts are convulsed over the misadventures of any one witnessed in horse-play or practical jokes. The degrading situations of a clown in the circus afford infinite amusement to such a person. He finds his comedy in buffoonery and laughs when some one is put to a disadvantage.

If we look into the matter closely we shall find the same thing where, perhaps, we should not expect to find it, namely, in the geniality and kindliness of humor. As the sympathetic feelings are developed in human nature we are not so prone to laugh at the misfortunes of others. A strong feeling of pity will defeat laughter. If we see a man by accident pitched head over heels into the water the ridiculousness of the situation does not appear till it is apparent that he is not hurt. Then, when he comes out, puffing and blowing, we laugh. Conscious of our power to help him, seeing that he is not seriously injured, we still enjoy observing that he is uncomfortable. In a more refined degree, the enjoyment of humor consists in this modified love of humiliating some one, wherein, as Dr. Bain says, " the indignity is disguised and, as it were, oiled by some kindly infusion such as would not consist with the unmitigated glee of triumphant superiority." " Sly digs," remote, disguised attacks, subtle suggestions of disparagement, wherein lies no real animosity, gratify at once the natural predatory inclinations and comport with the superior control of the sympathetic sentiments.

The fact that different things are comical to different people is readily explained from what has gone before. It depends upon a man's mental constitution whether or not he will laugh. A writer in the *Spectator* observes that because a refined man will not laugh at buffoonery, but will at a finely wrought epigram of Sydney Smith, it does not follow that he sees no joke in the former, but only a very little joke, for which he does not care, because he finds others so much better. It is the difference between *vin ordinaire* and *Château Lafitte*.

The circumstances, however, have much to do with laughter. When they are such as to involve constraint the sense of the ludicrous is aroused by more insignificant things. A dog trotting up the aisle in the midst of a church service excites merriment because of the very fact that laughter is out of place and propriety demands that it shall not be indulged. In a court of justice a poor joke will go farther and have more effect than in general conversation, for the reason that the ordinary severity and solemnity of the proceedings tire the participants or spectators and they are glad of the slightest relief. As Dr.

Bain says: " The mirthful is the aspect of ease, freedom, abandon, and animal spirits. The serious is constituted by labor, difficulty, and the necessities of our position. . . . It is always a gratifying deliverance to pass from the severe to the easy side of affairs, and the comic conjunction is one form of the transition." *

Whatever be the varying causes of laughter, or the feelings which constitute a sense of the ludicrous, the relief is always relief from a mental tension. There is a dissipation of concentrated energy without effort, a restoration of equilibrium which is comfortable and exhilarating. Mr. Spencer calls attention to the fact that the discharge of surplus feeling which results from the perception of a " descending incongruity " pervades the nervous system of the viscera, stimulating the internal organs as well as the muscles, the heart and the stomach coming in for a good part of the overflow. It thus is true that mirth assists digestion, and the man of jollity is not a dyspeptic.† No doubt this is the case within limitations. The sparkle of wit, the pleasantry of humor, the indulgence in the comic, produce a pleasurable state of emotion highly desirable to cultivate.

As in life, so in fictitious literature, representative of life. A story can be written which

---

* " Emotions and Will," ch. xiv.
† " Physiology of Laughter."

will interest, even if the comic or ludicrous do
not appear.   But, unless it be a short story, the
absence generally will be felt.   Like love, laughter
is a universal experience, occurring all the time
and in a great variety of situations.   With many
characters moving through different scenes there
must be sometimes and somewhere mirth-provok-
ing conditions and circumstances.   To leave out
and ignore such indicates a defect in artistic skill.
The drama of life represented is imperfect.   In
addition to this, the failure of interest from monotony is much more apt to occur where the amus-
ing is wanting.   Thus the writer who refuses to
use the ludicrous as a solvent for the concentrated
intensity of emotion he has developed through his
narration will find that presently he cannot arouse
powerful emotion at all, and his attempts will
only result in boring and fatiguing instead of
interesting his readers.   The exhibition of the
comic tends to the conservation of interest by
relieving monotony and removing the painful
strain of sympathetic attention.

It should be observed, though, that these beneficial effects may be entirely nullified by too con-
tinuous or frequent attempts to introduce the
ludicrous into a story.   Jokes, or ridiculous situations, get to be as tiresome as too serious depictions.   Comic books, wholly given up to laughter
excitation, are generally very tedious.   The professional humorist is apt to become a bore and a

nuisance. To sustain interest variety in the mental movement is required, and even if a writer be gifted with extraordinary brilliancy in wit or humor, it is always well for him not to be as funny as he can, and not to keep up his fun too long.

10

CHAPTER XII.

IT may now be expedient to consider the whole problem presented in connection with the general theme, to summarize the results attained, and to ascertain what questions remain to be asked and answered, as well as to determine what special branches of the subject require further treatment.

At the outset we limited the term *Fiction* to prose composition in the form of the story, tale, or novel; such limitation, however, being for the purposes of this essay and in accordance with usage, although a broader application of the word may be quite legitimate. We found our starting-point in the fact that people read fiction. If novels were not read and readable we should not have them. The first general query then presented itself: What is it in a story which interests the reader and holds his attention? In answer to this we found that interest is only another name for pleasure derived from the reading, that the source of such pleasure may be æsthetic, scientific, or moral, and that the three may contribute to the general effect in varying proportions. We may behold something beautiful, we may acquire knowledge, and we may have our moral sentiments and our conduct beneficially affected by the perusal of a book of fiction. For any one or all of these reasons we may be pleased with it.

We further noted that fiction is a representation of human experience, or that of beings with like faculties to those of men. The question then arose: Is not that the most interesting and the most perfect work which most exactly and accurately reproduces a section of such experience as it actually occurs? The answer to this query we found to cover a wide range of discussion. Among other things, we saw that experience itself involves a selective process, combining details into one whole in which the general impression prevails and to which the particulars are subordinated. Hence in the story, assembling details without careful attention to the general effect and plan is fatal to interest, except it be a scientific one. If we cater to this kind and foster it, we presently find ourselves leaving behind the realm of art and passing into that of science. Under the sway of the latter the tendency must be to eliminate fictitious literature. Exact truth is the ideal, and the story is only an imperfect mode of expression, suited to those minds which are not able to assimilate bald scientific statements. It is only the administration of wholesome medicine by a sugarcoated pill. As people grow better educated, the

tale or romance ought to disappear.   Art becomes
extinguished as no longer necessary.

If we desire to preserve and develop the æsthetic interests, then, and the moral as well, the
selective activities must be brought into play.   If
we represent experience, accuracy and exactness
are necessary, but a skill in combination and construction is just as important as correct copying
of nature.   There must be an ideal to direct the
work.   Under this direction choice is made of the
things to be reproduced, and the hand is guided
in accomplishing the reproduction.   The result is
a whole which is true to nature in its details, but
in which those details have been gathered, put together, and connected in an organic relation by a
creative power.

We thus saw that "naturalism," if adopted as
the governing theory of novelistic construction,
would impose a limitation upon such construction
quite inadmissible—a limitation which literature
never has endured and never will submit to, and
which would be destructive of this particular form
of literary production.   Its use is disciplinary and
preparatory, and, as such, of great value.   The
artist must be able to reproduce nature accurately,
and hence must be thoroughly acquainted with
nature's anatomy.   He must be trained, he must
learn how to use his eye and his hand, and, if
necessary, be a long while learning.   But when he
has learned, his work is not done ; the field is only

just opened to him. Nor must he allow himself to think that the memoranda of his dissections are to be the final product of his energy.

Inasmuch as conclusions respecting " realism," or "naturalism," and "idealism," or " romanticism," cannot furnish a full explanation of interest in a story, and since there must always be a selection of objects of interest from a great number of uninteresting things in experience, we found it necessary to pursue the inquiry further as to what does interest a reader. We learned that whatever interests people in real life holds their attention in fiction. An exhibition of power or force in action or resistance, especially human energy, will command that attention. Conflict and triumph, achievements under difficulties, suffering and conduct under pain, love and its manifestations, furnish material for the story-teller to construct an interesting narrative. Individual development in its environment, and social development through the action and reaction of its controlling forces, both supply legitimate subjects for the novelist's art. Beyond this the special tastes of the reader will determine whether or not he be pleased. War and cruelty will delight some, peace and kindliness others. Political movements will commend themselves to certain readers, novels of " manners " and social movements will gratify a different class. Since the things of contemporaneous interest principally occupy men's minds, moulding their thoughts and governing their feelings, that story will have the most readers which embodies and reproduces some phase of current life. For like reasons, portraitures of universal traits in human character attract and hold the attention.   And if there be in the minds of people generally an under-lying thought or belief struggling for expression, the novelist who understands and brings it out is sure of success.

Once more, we observed that relaxation of the strain of attention was important to a sustained interest, and that while change of scenes and variety of action would often accomplish a good deal in this direction, it was highly essential now and then to dissipate more thoroughly the sympa-thetic emotion aroused and concentrated by the narrative.   Therefore, the excitation of laughter by the representation of comic or ludicrous situa-tions, or by suggestions of them, is a most valu-able means of preventing fatigue in the reading of a story and of freshening the reader's pleasure in its development.   Wit and humor thus become of great consequence in the art of the novelist.

Now that we have investigated the sources of interest in a fictitious literary construction, and shown (according to our lights) what makes a story interesting, the further question arises : Should everything that is interesting to anybody be made the subject of the constructive writer's art ? This is not a question of " naturalism " or " romanticism," though sometimes it is esteemed to be so. It is a question of the relative importance of the æsthetic, the scientific, and the moral elements which, as we have seen, may enter into the interest of a work of fiction. Antagonisms may here arise which affect very decidedly the whole theory of artistic construction. That which is æsthetically pleasing may be immoral; that which is unscientific may be artistic; that which is moral may be repulsive as æsthetically considered. Again, the minds of different persons are so differently constituted that what seems moral to one may appear immoral to another; what gives æsthetic pleasure here may fail to do so there. If on any of the grounds specified a story is interesting to one, but is reprobated by another, is there any proper restriction of the exercise of creative skill in the interest of the community, and, if so, to what extent and in what cases?

It will readily be seen that we have presented the most serious problem connected with fiction in literature. A conflict is always raging over this question of the relations of the æsthetic and moral. Works of art are all the time suffering condemnation on account of their alleged immorality. On the other hand, if a story be written to subserve a moral purpose it is apt to be criticised as stupid and inartistic. Opposite judgments of books are formed by different people according as they follow æsthetic or moral standards. It is highly important that he who wishes to become a story-writer should understand exactly what he is about when he forms the plan of his tale ; shall appreciate how far he is appealing to each of the three great interests in a work of fiction, and how far he may disregard one for the sake of the other. It is also desirable for the reader, in order to form a just estimate of a book, to know what canons may be laid down by which properly to measure its value. We shall, therefore, devote ourselves now to a consideration of the questions just suggested. After answering them as well as we may be able, we shall be in a position to give such final conclusions respecting both the construction and the criticism of a work of fiction as may be needed to complete this essay.

CHAPTER XIII.

ART, MORALS, AND SCIENCE.

It is indispensable to a clear comprehension of the theory of art that we keep before us the truth, already fully developed in earlier pages, that essentially all art is creation. This is as true of what is termed reproductive or imitative art as it is of any other. A work of art is a product of the constructive power of the human mind, introduced as a new thing into the objective world. As such it is something done in realization of an ideal. In appreciating the work it is necessary for the observer to understand to some degree the ideal. He must be able to see what the artist had in mind in order to judge of the resultant product. If, then, it be well done, according to an ideal apprehended by the criticising mind, there is certainly aroused an æsthetic pleasure, greater or less according to the degree of excellence. This last may depend upon a variety of causes, in all of which, however, the difficulty of the achievement is an important element. That which the most of men cannot do elicits admiration; much more that which artists generally are unable to achieve.

The reader will remember the remark of Arréat, before quoted, to the effect that the true æsthetic idea in work is that of difficulty conquered, and which seems to have been conquered freely, or for the sake of the conquest.   Wherever this appears an æsthetic emotion is produced, independently of the subject-matter of the work itself. We say : Here is a fine thing, showing great power and genius.

It is quite true, therefore, that an artistic creation may give pleasure in itself, because it is æsthetic, irrespective of any scientific or moral value. In order, however, to get at the bottom of the matter, the question must be asked : What is the æsthetic pleasure? Is it in itself good or not? This last question we answered in the affirmative in Chapter V., and in the same connection made whatever investigation we were able into the nature of the pleasure we term æsthetic. In the light of what we found we must be prepared to admit that a work of art, æsthetically pleasing, justifies its own existence ; and since it exists for all, not perishing with the using, " a joy forever," it has a social and thus a moral value, *because* it is æsthetic, and so far forth as it is so.

If this were all that is to be said the solution of the problem would be easy. In reality it is much more complicated. We remember one of the essential elements of æsthetic pleasure to be that the object which produces it shall be so exhibited that the disagreeable is thrown into the background or minimized. And we also noted that what is disagreeable to one is not to another. If, however, something which is unpleasant is brought before or suggested to the mind, the æsthetic impression is weakened. A work of art under such circumstances is less beautiful. According to the temperament of individuals, defects in form and repulsive suggestions of the subject-matter alike impair the æsthetic interest, because they violate an æsthetic law. The æsthetic value is depreciated.

Morality is a necessity of social life. The relations of human beings to each other are organic, and conduct must be regulated to some degree by every one with reference to others. Under the pressure of the social situation of mankind, ideals of duty grow and a moral sensibility is developed. As this sense increases in power, it tends more and more to dominate the whole mental nature and to control conduct. That which is right is approved and that which is wrong is repugnant. The moral consequences of actions are regarded closely and educational influences become of importance. Moral men and women please and the immoral are displeasing. Our sympathies are with righteousness and our aspirations are toward moral ideals.

Such being the case, it is evident that the growth of a moral sensibility must modify the

æsthetic sensibility.   If a work of art offends the
moral susceptibilities strongly, its beauty departs
from it.   It may be well executed, but it dis-
pleases, shocks, horrifies.   It is ugly, not beautiful, and we turn away from it with repugnance.
A work of art it may be, but not of high art.   It
does not fully satisfy the conditions of æsthetic
approval.   It must inevitably follow from these
considerations that the sense of beauty and artistic excellence is not independent of the moral
sense, because the latter helps to form the artistic
ideal.   Regard for it is a condition of æsthetic
pleasure.   Equally inevitable is the conclusion
that it is impossible to eliminate the moral from
æsthetic judgments and to divorce morality and
art.   If, then, we say that a work of real art is
therefore moral, true as the statement may be, it
does not exclude the further truth that the moral
element has been necessary to make that work a
truly artistic product.

There are various modes in which ethical sentiments influence people in the way of affecting
their æsthetic appreciation.   Of these modes two
general classes may roughly be made: the one, of
the effects the work may have upon conduct and
character; the other, in the revelation made of the
mind and character of the artist himself.   Considering the first of these, we are offended if an essentially false view of human experience is presented by which people would be misled to their

detriment. Arguments in support of evil courses by showing light or beneficial consequences flowing therefrom are of this order. Unless such arguments are overcome and a proper balance restored, the moral sensibilities are painfully disturbed. We are displeased with the work because of its untruth, and the injury which is possible to result from this want of fidelity to truth. Our moral (and also, in this case, our scientific) sentiments cause us to regard the art-product as imperfect. It fails as to fitness, proportion, order, keeping, congruity. It is not well done. Oftentimes, to be sure, this moral assertion is very unreasonable and unjustifiable. It has sway because of the low degree of the individual's intelligence. Of this we need not at present take account; we are only remarking one of the cases in which the ethical sentiment makes itself felt. Another illustration, and one exhibiting moral emotion in its purity, is found in the indignation which is excited when distinctly evil passions are encouraged and stimulated, or are thought to be, by a work of art. Where devilishness seems to be dominant we lose all patience and become blind to everything else. The impression may even be that of ugliness, against which beauties that some might readily see have no countervailing force.

In all these cases there is a reversion to the artist and a lower opinion formed of him, which still further impairs the work. We think he is not skilful, not clever, not a man of genius, else his judgment would have been truer. He would have seen that he was presenting a partial or one-sided view. He would have been conscious that the observer, unless of inferior intelligence, could not take pleasure in what he produces. He is deficient in his understanding of what constitutes good art, he fails to read human character, and he is unable to form those ideals which give the fullest inspiration for artistic essays. Thus, it being impossible, as we have noted, to remove the personality of the artist from estimates of his work, moral sentiments may so powerfully influence people as to form and control their æsthetic judgments and artistic sense from despising or condemning the author as well as his production.

This seems rather extreme, but many of us have seen instances quite bearing out the above assertion. Prejudice is blind, and strong feeling will result in a blinding antipathy. But even though increase of intelligence produces a more just and evenly balanced mind, artists must not expect that moral considerations will cease to influence judgments upon works of art. This never can be, for the reasons stated :

" Truth and Good are one,
   And Beauty dwells with them, and they in her,
   With like participation." *

---

* Akenside.

What can and ought to be done is to so educate the human mind as to create a true moral perspective, to cause the whole field of life and conduct to be surveyed and things to be seen in their true relations, to secure a correct estimate of the degree of morality or immorality in particular things. Then calm judgment will take the place of that moral fury which is itself immoral, and the mere fact that one's prejudices are offended will not suffice for the condemnation of a work of art which has many merits in the eyes of him who has a wider comprehension and a deeper insight.

The true philosophy of this subject is found in recognizing the general correspondence and interdependence of ideals of Beauty, Truth, and Goodness. As I have remarked elsewhere,* the same ideal may be an ideal of truth, beauty, or goodness, according as it is viewed ; that is to say, the same mental picture or fiction may serve the purpose of a scientific ideal; of awakening pleasure, or of an emotive ideal; of inspiring volition, or a volitional ideal ; and it is not easy to say in what degree each influences the others. For the impressions of beauty, truth, and utility are often demanded. The utility of an object, in fact, often determines its beauty, as we see prominently exemplified in architecture, where a pillar, an arch, or a foundation is totally destitute of æsthetic

---

* " System of Psychology," ch. lii., vol. ii.

effect unless it subserve the ends of the edifice. Very few things can be cited as good which do not carry with them the value of truth. Scientific ideals lie at the basis of ideals of goodness. Again, the utility of some things depends upon their beauty, while the members of the whole class of æsthetic ideals have utility as being objects of pleasurable contemplation, and thus ends to be sought. Scientific ideals being peculiarly related to cognition, æsthetic ideals to emotion, and moral ideals to volition and action, their close connection and interfusion is necessitated from the psychological interdependence of cognition, feeling, and volition themselves.

After these general remarks, we will proceed to a more particular consideration of that branch of artistic production which is the subject of this essay. What has been said as to the impossibility of avoiding the influence of moral sentiments applies with special force to this department of art. As we saw in the opening chapters, not only are moral and scientific values found in stories, but works of fiction are often written with a defi-nite moral or scientific purpose. Indeed, in the minds of some its didactic end has frequently been considered the sole *raison d'être* of the novel. These facts should not be lost sight of, though, happily, broader views generally prevail. Yet, while the reading public does not require that a story be written with a moral purpose, there is prevalent a strong feeling that it shall not be immoral or of unhealthy educational tendency. If it is so, its artistic merit is diminished.

It is quite certain that no universal rules can be laid down, upon the topic of moral effect, as to the selection or exclusion of subjects, nor as to the method of treatment when once a subject is chosen. People do not think alike ; they are differently susceptible to influences, and there is no uniformity of standard either of ethical or educational principles. Accordingly, in our discussion we shall examine a few of the leading particulars in fiction composition with respect to which the charge of immoral influence or effect is likely to be brought. These cases we shall consider, with a view of ascertaining how far such a charge can be substantiated, and the nature of the effect itself.

In the first place, we should notice such stories as by their plot, by the conversation of their characters, or by the interjected sentiments of the author, assault existing religious or political institutions. No doubt in all cases the supporters of such institutions would denounce works of this character as both immoral and criminal. The latter, indeed, they may be when not the former. A crime is not necessarily immoral. Criminality is a creation of law. Reading the Bible may be made a crime, but it would hardly be considered an act against morality. In Virginia people were once actually convicted of and punished for the crime

of teaching slaves to read the Bible. Whatever
by law is made an offence against the State is
criminal, but not therefore immoral. Reproba-
tion of a book because it is a protest against existing authority may thus be very severe, and yet
it could not be considered of immoral influence,
except on theories which identify morality with
submission to authority. Such theories prevail,
however, at some times and places, and have pre-
vailed very extensively in the past. Through
them sentiments are created which prevent artistic value from being recognized and tend to
repress genius.

Living in an enlightened age, and in a country
where speech is free, I do not propose to take up
space to argue in favor of the right to criticise the
established, either in politics or religion. Though
we must allow the melancholy fact that prejudice
does render men both deaf and blind, we may
safely maintain, wherever we find on close analysis that the gravamen of the accusation of immorality against a novel lies in its opposition to
the domination of authority as such, that the
charge has no foundation. In such a case, we
ought to pray that men may become enlightened,
so that they may see the truth and by the truth
may be made free from a debasing slavery fatal
to honesty and the truest morality. If, then, we
should be told that a story is " bad," and on inquiry
should discover that our critic means it is bad be-

cause an argument might be drawn from it against monarchy, or republicanism, against the Romish Church, or episcopacy, or presbyterianism, or agnosticism, we may safely discard the adverse judgment and try to eliminate from our minds whatever bias may lurk there by reason of our own predilections. Art cannot be understood or appreciated without a broad and judicial mind. We need not hesitate to say, therefore, that any book condemned as pernicious, nominally or really, on the ground that it is subversive of established authority, should not for that reason be set aside. Such an objection should rather be wholly ignored ; and unless we are able to ignore it, we are not competent to pass judgment on the work. Its morality or immorality has nothing to do with such considerations, much less its excellence as a work of art.

Let us now turn to questions of the depiction of that which is conceded to be evil, apart from any declaration of authority. From our present consideration we will leave out illustrations of the sexual passion for separate treatment a little later. We shall have remaining those promptings of a wicked nature which lead to offences of various sorts against life, liberty, and property. Of these murder is the chief, and may be taken as a typical example. Is the representation of the unlawful killing of human beings and the circumstances leading thereto immoral? If it be, and we are to abolish tragedy in fiction, certainly a large amount of romantic literature would have to be destroyed, and with it a great many masterpieces. Surely bloodthirstiness cannot be ignored in human life, and if the novelist makes his selection of important characters from the cruel and the murderous, he will at least be likely to arouse that interest which monstrosity evokes. Besides, the development of incident issuing at last in murder is usually startling enough to hold the reader's attention on the principle of the *idée fixe*.

The immoral effect of tales involving bloodshed does not come from the facts introduced but rather from their coloring. If murder be dignified and justified, and if a murderer be painted as a hero, undoubtedly an influence is exerted over the mind of an immature reader formative of a false ideal of character. The same influence may obtain also with the more mature, though in less degree. Walter Scott, perhaps, is the most successful of any writer in making homicide charming, and in elevating thugs to the rank of demi-gods. His heroes, from Richard Cœur de Lion through the list, are chiefly brutal ruffians, over whom the false splendor of the ideals of chivalry has cast a glamour. The highest and noblest sentiments are ascribed to men who would not hesitate to slay each other in a quarrel over some trifling matter of "honor." They have not the faintest idea of a complete all-around, comprehensive morality.

Yet they are so presented as to claim admiration, and to receive it from most readers. It would startle people to hear Sir Walter's novels charged with immorality, and it would be very difficult for the average reader to consider them as obnoxious to such a charge. The reason for this state of things is, I opine, the remoteness of the danger of any one being corrupted by Scott's representations of character, coupled with his admirable style of depiction, and the scientific interest aroused in the manner and morals of a departed age. People are not incited to murder and robbery by reading the poems of Homer or the books of the Pentateuch, though, in both, these crimes be praised, and indeed commanded by divine authority. The environment is entirely different from that of the reader, and while the moral sense of disapproval may sometimes be stirred, it is at once balanced by the reflection that the reader lives in happier and better times, where violence is no longer prevalent, and where, if it occur, the offender will encounter the prison and the hangman. Our Rob Roys of the present day may have just as excellent traits as their prototype, but the condition of civilization is such that they cannot be heroes—unless it be in Kentucky.

The danger of immoral effect from tales of blood is much increased where the scene is laid in circumstances so nearly like the surroundings of the reader as to influence his own conduct insensibly,

to convince him that homicide is justifiable and
that private revenge is proper, and indeed manly.
In Mr. Marion Crawford's story, " Greifenstein,"
the owner of a castle, living contentedly enough
with his wife, receives a visit from a brother from
whom he had been estranged. Over their wine at
dinner the discovery is made that the wife was the
woman who had formerly married the visitor and
deserted him ; whereupon the two brothers conclude that the only thing to do is to strangle the
woman and then each commit suicide. All this
is successfully accomplished. Of course, the men
do these things from the highest motives. It is
morally necessary to choke the wife and shoot
themselves. The author does not justify this,
but he presents us with two very respectable men
who do. Mr. Edgar Saltus, in " Mr. Incoul's Misadventure," describes Mr. Incoul as taking his
revenge upon a supposed adulterous wife by giving her a sleeping draught, then turning on the gas
after closing the windows of her chamber and lock-
ing the door with the key on the inside by means
of a pair of pincers used from without. Then,
after the funeral, he goes about his avocations,
relieved that he has got through with a disagreeable business; his " misadventure " having been
his marriage, and the unpleasant necessity of having to murder his wife—an unpleasantness, however, that a gentleman may have to encounter and
endure, and for which he should be prepared as

for any other of the *petites misères de la vie.* M.
de Maupassant, in " L'Ordonnance," finds a climax
in the colonel, after the suicide of his wife, driven
thereto by double adultery on her part (and after
the receipt of a letter written by her before death
setting forth the details of her sins), calling in his
offending orderly and shooting him down instantly
in the tent. The victim was a cur, who had induced the wife to comply with his wishes by threatening to tell the husband who her real lover was.
Another very respectable man is presented as committing murder because it was the proper thing
to do, the circumstances being such as to make
sympathy with the murdered man almost impossible.

Without more illustrations — multitudes of
which will occur to every one—we find educated,
sensible, refined people constantly exhibited in
novels as committing crimes of violence from alleged moral motives, superior to the law. Ideal
justice, of which they are the ministers, takes away
the guilt and removes the stigma. That such
arguments as are used to support deeds of personal revenge are sophistical is clear enough to a
well-balanced mind. Lynch law even is more justifiable, for that is a social, not an individual, act.
That people do entertain sentiments approving of
the " cheap justice of the shot-gun " is unfortu-
nately true. All the more dangerous, then, is the
influence of that fictitious literature which pict-

ures deeds of murderous criminality as something likely to happen naturally in the life of the ordinary civilized human being. Such literature may not incite the reader to indulge in homicide himself, but it very likely will cause him to vote for acquittal the next time he sits on a jury trying a man who has committed murder from " high motives."

Where there is a strong reaction in the reader's mind, as he peruses a tale of the character we are considering, little harm is done. Then he condemns the book. He is disposed to think it inferior as a work of art, his moral perceptions dominating. But if he reads more of the same sort, his moral feeling is weakened. If the most of the stories he reads are of similar nature, he will come to enjoy them, and the ultimate effect upon him will be precisely that of bad company, influencing less or more, according to his strength or weakness of character. The youth or the man of low intelligence, who is unable to weigh arguments, is of course likely to be injured most. There can be no doubt that " dime novels " and exciting tales of bloody adventure generally are among the causes of crimes of violence. These, indeed, are of the lowest hell. Yet their superiors have much for which they are answerable.

If, now, we proceed to consider the morality of minute descriptions of vice and crime, we shall find, I apprehend, that the " naturalists " have at last the advantage of a good argument. They can say with much truth, that if vice is to be revealed in a story it should be exactly and accurately presented; the cancer should be shown with all its roots; that then its hatefulness would be a powerful deterrent. Still, omitting the sexual, naturalistic accounts of the horrible nature of evil dispositions and deeds certainly will not be likely to allure. The real objection to details of vice is an æsthetic rather than a moral one. They are so repulsive that they destroy the artistic effect. It is difficult to understand how Dostoyevsky's " Crime and Punishment," for example, can have aught but a moral effect ; yet the work is by no means pleasant reading. The same thing is true of many of the war scenes in ´Tolstoï's " War and Peace." But it is the very minuteness of analysis which takes away the chance of evil effect.

If the hideousness of crime stands forth saliently, the inevitable wretchedness of the perpetrator and the utter wreck of his energies and hopes for life are made plain, the whole current of the reader's mind is set against evil courses. Such is the net result of works like the masterpieces of Balzac —" Père Goriot," " Eugénie Grandet," " César Birotteau," "Le Peau de Chagrin." George Eliot, no doubt, thought the first of these " hateful," because it presented such an unpleasant picture of human character. She would not have called it an im-

moral book. The moral of " Le Peau de Chagrin "
is obvious and impressive. The portrayals by
Dickens of besotted vice and brutal wickedness
can have no tendency to make people adopt as
models of character such vile specimens of humanity as he sets before his readers. No one reading
a story like Mrs. Anne Sheldon Coombs's " A
Game of Chance " would ever thereby become en-
amoured of the stock-speculation so commonly
destructive in modern life. We must conclude,
therefore, that if a novel deal with evil, realistic
or naturalistic description is in general not to be
regarded as objectionable on the score of vicious
tendency. It may be unpleasant and have the
depressing effect that the observation of depravity
has always upon the virtuous mind ; on this point
we shall have more to say later. But at all events
the book is not otherwise immoral by reason of
these things.

It must be allowed, however, that the foregoing
remarks need qualification by the exception which
we have all along made. Minute accounts of the
workings of the sexual passion are to be placed
in a somewhat different category. We are thus
brought to a topic of great importance in the
philosophy of fiction, a subject which in recent
times is engaging the attention of writers and
readers more extensively than ever before, because
of the increasing boldness of masters of fiction-
writing in selecting and treating phases of human

experience not hitherto deemed fit for the novelist's art. Teachers of morality are generally appalled by this freedom, and condemnations of literary licentiousness are everywhere heard. It behooves us, then, to examine with some care this phenomenon of literary production.

In Chapter IX. we remarked the fact that the chief cause of interest in erotic description is the stimulation of sexual appetite. This is the reason why minute depictions of the course of sex-relations cannot be regarded in the same light, morally speaking, as details of the working of vicious passion of a predatory nature. They tend to awaken, develop, and intensify an organic appetite, the means for gratifying which are everywhere found in social life. If, then, such gratification be immoral and dangerous, so are books which encourage it. Gautier's " Mademoiselle de Maupin " is one of the most beautiful and charming works of an erotic character; but it seems useless for any one to attempt to deny that the interest in that work comes essentially from the excitation of sexual feeling, more or less strong according to temperament and age. The delightful style, the many scenes and descriptions of a highly artistic character, contribute to the general effect; for, as we have also observed in a former chapter, the æsthetic and the sexual are closely related. In the particular work in question we have carnal amatory passion idealized and made beautiful.

Let us contrast with this " Justine " and " Juliette " of the Marquis de Sade, a monomaniac in
sexual diabolisms. These books—*livres-à-clef*—
portray the appetite as leading to and finding its
satisfaction in the most horrible and abominable
cruelties. Intermixed with the narrative is a
quantity of sophistical philosophizing which could
only have come from a half-crazed brain. It is
difficult to see what there is in such narratives as
these to attract any but the most brutal natures.
One would hardly think that accounts of erotic
association with hellish circumstances, torture, and
the scenes of the slaughter-house, would incite anybody to debauchery. Only abnormal beings would
derive any satisfaction from such accounts as are
found in " Justine " and " Juliette." We should
naturally call the books most outrageously immoral ; but there is room for questioning whether
their effect on character and conduct would be as
bad as that of " Mademoiselle de Maupin." I do
not wish to be understood as asserting that the
latter is a worse book than the former. I only
suggest the argument that Gautier's masterpiece
will endure in literature, while the horrid tales of
the Marquis de Sade never can, save for the interest of the curious. If feeding this particular appetite æsthetically is to be reprobated, I think we
must concede that much more nourishment in this
line is afforded by " Mademoiselle de Maupin "
than by " Justine." The one is to most people

æsthetically superb; the other, æsthetically considered, is detestable. What shall we say as to
the morality?

Those who wish to defend the erotic in novels
will be forced by the exigencies of fact and logic to
take a much bolder line of argument if they insist
upon their position. To say that "to the pure all
things are pure" will not meet the case. Some
cynic has parodied this expression by the assertion
that "to the pure all things are nasty." No doubt
a virgin of forty-five will see or imagine salacious-
ness in a novel much quicker than a married
woman of thirty. Old bachelors, too, of ascetic
characters get very morbid in these matters. But
whatever the condition of the reader, it is foolish to
urge that a warmly colored, artistically presented
story of sex-affiliations will generally please merely
on account of its abstract beauty. Its beauty will
be heightened if not formed by erotic stimulation;
very refined it may be, but still, after all, consti-
tuting the basis of appreciation. If this be so, the
artist who justifies "the nude in literature" will
have to take the ground that the excitation of the
sexual appetite is not so harmful as has been
claimed by ascetic moralists, and that its gratification is, to a greater extent than has been allowed,
a matter of personal choice and right, instead of
social morality. No doubt the author who asserted
this would raise a hornet's nest about his ears;
but it is much better to look into the matter pro-

foundly rather than superficially.   It is wiser to
present the question squarely and discuss it can-
didly than to put ourselves off with hypocrisies
and equivocations.   This cant about reading erotic
books for the " style," the " moral lessons " from
the vagaries of vice, the " æsthetic form," the
thousand-and-one reasons except the true one, is
very tiresome and disgusting.   They are read by
the general public because they exhibit the movements of a powerful human appetite which the
readers possess, which sensibly or insensibly enters
into the life and affects the conduct of those
readers, and which is pleasantly stimulated by
imagination and fictitious narrative.

It is not my purpose to enter into the discussion
of what is and what is not true sexual morality
and immorality.   I have considered these questions in another work, which I expect to publish.
But there are some things which should be said
apropos of the present topic, in order that we may
understand the meaning, and the bearings upon
literature, of the depiction of erotic sentiment.
The first of these is that the prevalence of such
portrayals is evidence of an increasing development of sentiment in the direction indicated in
the last paragraph, and away from the old ascetic
standards.   The latter required that no mention
should be made of the promptings of the sexual
passion, or its influence upon character, or even its
relations to love.   Irregular sexual associations

must not be dwelt upon, and their mention in a
story is án objection to it. I personally know of
a certain novel having been rejected by a leading
publishing house in New York for the sole reason
(as stated) that it referred to one of its characters
keeping a mistress, the latter, however, not being
brought forward prominently in the work. This
is almost as bad as another instance within the
writer's knowledge, wherein an ancient fossil, who
for many years occupied the position of reader for
a large publishing firm, rejected a story as immoral because its opening chapter described a
party of young men at Delmonico's, who got hila-
rious over their cups before they left. Both of
these stories were discarded on the ascetic principle that to recognize vice is to favor, and to
ignore is the best way of extinguishing it. I have
often wondered why intelligent *roués* should not
see the value to them of this policy of non-obser-
vation and silence. How much more to their advantage is it when society considers certain things
as impossible, and how much wider the field for
their operations. But we cannot avoid asking
people of ascetic proclivities some day to put on
spectacles of a little higher power, to look on the
world as it is, and then seriously ask themselves
the question whether knowledge may not after all
be better than innocence for the cause of sound
morals.

The Gallic freedom of expression in regard to

matters of sex-relations is, no doubt, quite shock-
ing to many Anglo-Saxons. Moreover, the French
believe in recognizing sex-pleasures as legitimate
ends in themselves, to be enjoyed for their own
sake, and not merely as means to providential
purposes.   Hence, these become, like all other
pleasures, the proper subjects of art. This also
is abominable to the Anglo-Saxon mind. But
it may well be doubted if the general family life
and morality of the French is any worse or on
any lower plane than the English. In London I
have noticed that a great many improper things
are done, even if nothing is said. In Paris, I am
inclined to the belief that fewer iniquities are committed, because such matters are talked and written about. Be that as it may, it cannot be denied
that the Frenchman likes to have adopted as the
subject of literary fiction matters of occurrence
which the Englishman would not at present toler-
ate from an author writing in his own language.
With the former, therefore, the erotic in life is as
much entitled to artistic and literary treatment as
any other phase of human experience.

In such a condition of sentiment as that which
the French display, questions of morality are
greatly modified. If the state of innocence be
once gone, a very complete education is the best
thing.   Hence a book like M. Alphonse Daudet's
" Sappho," in the midst of modern French literature, cannot properly be considered as other than

moral. The author's dedication to his sons when they shall have reached the age of twenty years indicates that he thought its educational influence beneficial. His judgment is no doubt correct. An American living in a country community, where an Arcadian simplicity prevails, would probably not have the book in his house, because he would esteem it dangerous. "Anna Karénina" surely cannot be regarded as encouraging vice, nor can Paul Lindau's "Lace," both of which deal with fatal consequences of adultery. Yet these last two are often condemned with the other, and for like reasons—the blessedness of ignorance.

American critics are complaining of the "Gallic taint" as conspicuous in recent American fiction to an alarming degree. A newspaper reviewer in a leading journal observes that "the French fiction of the day, with its ever-increasing morbidness and impurity, and its diaphanous pretences of art for art's sake, has been silently absorbed, and with a growth in eagerness bespeaking decadent ethical principles." It is quite true that a number of tales of the erotic type have appeared within a few years; but it must not be forgotten that the condition of American literature is such that a few books of this kind will make more stir than a multitude of a less unusual character. Probably this is one chief reason why the authors and publishers issue them. It is worth considera-

12

ble to have a book savagely condemned on this
score. Present sales are of more consequence
than posthumous fame. But it is not to be supposed that the tastes of people in the United
States have changed radically in the last decade;
and if in about that time nearly a million copies
of E. P. Roe's novels have found a market, we
need not be troubled for the present over the
spread of Gallic poison. Nevertheless, we might
as well make up our minds that American fictitious literature has lost its virgin innocence. It
will be far better to conquer our squeamishness
and cheerfully allow that there is such a thing as
passion, that there are in the world irregularities
of sex-relations, and that all phases of human experience may supply material for the novelist, if his
treatment of them be decent. If public sentiment
allows more liberty, we shall have stronger and
better works of more ethical as well as æsthetic
value. For the sake of this we can afford to tol-
erate an occasional erotic genius, satisfied that in
the multitude of educational influences the harm
he can do is very limited.

Professor H. H. Boyesen, of Columbia College,
New York, performed a most excellent service in an
article published in the *Forum*, in which he discussed
the reason why in America we have as he considers no great novelists. He thinks it is because
stories are constructed on the theory that they must
be suited to the educational needs of the Young

Person, particularly the Young Girl. Hence, " a weak lemonade mixture, harmless and mildly ex-hilarating, adapted for the palate of *ingénues*, is poured out in a steady stream from our presses, and we all drink it, and from patriotic motives declare it to be good." There is sound truth in these remarks, though the facts be not creditable to us. The idea that a story-writer is bound to write nothing but what every young person, how-ever weak his or her moral fibre, may safely read, would, if carried out, reduce fictitious writing to the category of Sunday-school books. Not but what a writer may devote himself entirely to the latter class of composition. But to declare that they are to exclude others or furnish the standard of novel-writing is ridiculous. . The healthy growth of a literature depends upon its freedom for expansion. Unwholesome books there may be, but there are unwholesome people. Of the two the latter are much worse, yet they are in the world about us, and our children see them and meet them without perceptible harm. If we do our duty in educating we can create in children a sound and healthy character based on knowledge instead of ignorance. The " sheltered life" theory as to both girls and boys is carried altogether too far. Knowledge must come some time ; better that it be acquired naturally and accurately when it is sought rather than to have formed in the mind a wrong " illusion " of life, as

M. de Maupassant calls it, by a process of that *suppressio veri,* which is to the young a *suggestio falsi.* When, in the last case, the Young Person becomes undeceived, when he does eat of the tree of knowledge, the shock to him is very great, and he is apt to lose all confidence both in learning and in human character. The other is much the better way. But, in any event, literature does not exist solely for children and youth, nor is the question of its morality or immorality to be settled exclusively by reference to the effect on them. Let their needs be considered, of course, but also let it be considered that grown people have rights. If milk be the proper food for babes, strong men should not be deprived of meat because the babes may sometimes get hold of it to their detriment.

One of the best discussions of this question of "the nude in literature" is found in an article published in the New York *World* * under that title, and written by Mr. George Cary Eggleston. I venture to quote a few sentences which, to my mind, express exactly the true doctrine of this difficult subject. He says: "The modern novelist must deal with modern life. If his work is to be of any value he must deal with it truthfully. It is not permitted to him, if he be a true artist or if his work is to have any value, to deal with one side of it, ignoring the existence of the other. He

---

* December 15, 1889.

must recognize fact and state it. If he does so with fidelity and with honest purpose, the result is good and for good ; if he does so, as many modern novelists have done, without fidelity, the result must be evil in every case.

. . . .

" Every fact of human life, every trait of human character, every possibility of human conduct is legitimate material for the use of the creative literary artist, and every such fact, trait, and possibility may be wholesomely or evilly employed, according as the purpose and method of its employment may determine. The trouble is that both in the popular judgment and in what is called 'literary criticism' there is a constant failure to discriminate between wholesome and unwholesome methods, between legitimate and illegitimate uses.

. . . .

" It is not a question of legitimacy of materials ; it is a question of the legitimacy of the uses made of them.

" All truths are wholesome if wholesomely treated, and if the art of fiction is not to fall into utter decay, this principle must be recognized by the critics and by the public. Failure to recognize it is the chief cause of the prevalence and success of evilly erotic fiction. It has the effect to silence the voices of those who wish to deal wholesomely with the unwholesome things of life, and turns over the most necessary materials of creative art to those whose foul minds desire only to misapply them. It is time for a sharp revision of judgments in a matter that vitally concerns the future of fictitious literature among us."

If we adopt Mr. Eggleston's canons for our standard we shall not reject novels because a mistress is introduced in them, nor because they show violations of the seventh commandment, nor because they recognize sexual passion in any form. We shall not restrict the artist as to his materials. But we shall look a little more closely than the French do to the manner in which he uses those materials. We shall have some regard for growing youth, even if we do not allow that literature exists only for them. We shall understand that the tendency of too naturalistic descriptions in this line is bad from a moral point of view and must be curtailed. Carried too far, if it cease to be immoral it may become æsthetically offensive. Then, as Mr. Henry James says, in his essay on Charles Baudelaire : " We are at a loss to know whether the subject pretends to appeal to our conscience or—we were going to say—to our olfactories. ' Le Mal,' we exclaim, ' you do yourself too much honor. This is not evil ; it is not the wrong ; it is simply the nasty ! ' "

For the novelist the difficulty would be, I suspect, to refrain from realistic descriptions if he once selects a topic which involves the effect of sex-appetite on conduct. If he is truly an artist it will be hard for him to content himself with what he will inevitably consider inadequate portrayal. Even if he so frame his story as to produce on the whole a highly moral effect, there will be scenes where he is tempted to paint vividly and color warmly. It is very possible, then, that the reader may feed his imagination on these scenes and fail to receive the general lesson. We have often noticed in public libraries portions of books dealing with or calling attention to some form of sexuality well-worn and soiled by finger-marks, when the rest of the volumes, innocent of such allusions, are left white and clean. Dr. O. W. Holmes * refers to this fact in discussing " Madame Bovary." He remarks of Flaubert's great novel: "That it has a serious lesson there is no doubt, if one will drink down to the bottom of the cup. But the honey of sensuous description is spread so deeply over the surface of the goblet that a large proportion of its readers never think of its holding anything else. All the phases of unhallowed passion are described in full detail. This is what the book is bought and read for by the great majority of its purchasers, as all but simpletons very well know." Yet there is much reason for Mr. James's thought the first time he read it, "that it would make the most useful of Sunday-school tracts." * Some of Swedenborg's works that treat of the reproductive activities furnish very good erotic reading; yet the moral and religious purpose (and general effect, if properly read) of these deliverances is perfectly evident, and for this his works are highly valued and Swedenborg himself held in great reverence by many moralists.

How, then, after these reflections, shall we answer the question asked a few pages back as to the morality of "Mademoiselle de Maupin"? I do not see how we can escape from the conclusion that its effect on character and conduct is naturally bad (and hence it is of immoral tendency), if we believe that the gratification of the sexual appetite is not to be considered a legitimate pleasure, to be enjoyed and cultivated for its own sake, irrespective of any particular ends or purposes to be subserved thereby.

But even if it be thus estimated, there arises also the question of temperance which must be met, and we discover that those people who would read such books with the most interest are the very ones most likely to be injuriously affected by the descriptions. On the other hand, it is to be said that after character is formed on the basis of chastity and continence, conduct would not be influenced, and the only effect is that æsthetic

---

* " French Poets and Novelists."

pleasure which is connected with manifestations of the sex-passion. Or, if the character be established on the ideas of the sybarite and voluptuary, it may be urged that the reader will be no worse for the reading and that he has a right to indulge his own tastes as he pleases, though his preferences are not ours. On the whole, therefore, we must conclude that, considered educationally, " Mademoiselle de Maupin" is dangerous, the more so on account of the beautiful style in which it is written; that otherwise it is good or bad on the moral side according to whether we believe in the ascetic or the epicurean view of the pleasures of sex-relations. In the former case a strong sentiment prevents us from allowing to such pleasures a legitimate æsthetic existence, denies that they may be made enjoyments for their own sake, and considers that they should be indulged only for race preservation. In the latter case, the more refined and beautiful such enjoyments be made to appear, the more they are brought under the principles of æsthetic government, the better. Associations of uncleanliness should on that theory be eliminated, and nakedness cease to be cause for shame, until those ideals and sentiments of which we have evidence as existing in Greece in the period of the fullest artistic development are again realized. Morality in such case becomes a matter of temperance and prudence, the obligations of which are imperative

enough, to be sure, but rest on a different foundation from those imposed by the ascetics.

For the sake of contrast let us look at a class of
novels of which Paul Heyse's " In Paradise " may
be taken as a type. This work does not deal in
sensuous description ; on the contrary, the intellectual and spiritual side of life is always uppermost. A little coterie of artists is brought together
and the work gives us their lives. They are
animated by the highest sentiments, the themes
and the tone of conversation are elevating, the
characters are by no means low. Yet at the end of
the work one of the ladies leaves her husband and
goes off to Italy to live with another man. This
is done after deliberation, with the full approval
of their friends, and they live contentedly and
happily forever afterward, no avenging Nemesis
disturbing their felicity. In taking this step they
have realized their ideals of life. Now, if we consider that such a course is inculcated by the story
as a laudable one, the moral or lesson is against
morality, save under the doctrine that marriage is
not a binding contract, but may be dissolved at the
will of either party. It may be said there is no
such lesson taught. The author simply exhibits a
picture. Such things happen among respectable
people, who have this peculiar " illusion " of life.
But in a story the " illusion " is apt to be regarded
as typical of what is, or as an ideal of what ought
to be. A society is constructed wherein modes of

life like those indicated are proper and apparently
conduce to happiness. The influence exerted may
not be very evident, but it is subtle and insinuat-
ing. The reader asks himself : Since excellent
people do these things, why may not I ? Or, is
not the social condition here described, after all,
better than our own ? If the reading of the book
aroused the earnest and sincere desire to answer
thoroughly and completely such queries as these,
no harm would result. The difficulty is, however,
that few readers will be impelled to such a course.
The most will receive the impression and be insensibly affected by it. They will adopt half-truths
as the whole ; they will generalize too broadly ;
the representation of this particular " illusion "
will prevent the formation of others ; they will
come to adopt it as their own and be content that
it become universal, not taking account of the
pains and penalties to individuals and to society.
The more nearly the reader identifies himself and
his social environment with that of the people in
the story who do wrong, the greater is the moral
danger. If these intellectual and delightful persons, whose tastes and habits are so like mine and
those of my friends, get along so comfortably and
satisfactorily, are not my good friend, Mrs. Pious-
in-Church, and myself rather slow creatures if we
fail to go and do likewise ? We might as well take
advantage of what life affords. In so doing we
may even satisfy a long-felt soul-aspiration and

come into a much fuller and more complete development of our whole moral nature !

Paul Heyse's elective affinity based on intellectual tastes and sympathies is a fair example of adultery according to German ideas. M. de Maupassant's " Bel-Ami " shows the French fashion— much more complicated and interlacing. In this latter novel, the " highly intellectual " and the " superior moral " do not appear. Still, the society in which the *dramatis personæ* move is a perfectly respectable one on the surface. " Bel-Ami " certainly would not demoralize the same class of minds that would be affected by " In Paradise," nor would it operate in the same way. The former would appeal to a Frenchman's interest—but I doubt much if a Frenchman is ever injured by books of this sort. They do not form his society ; they are rather a product of it ; and the masculine mind at any rate has received its own impressions from real experience as soon as it receives them from books, if not before ; while young French girls and women are under close surveillance as to their reading. Nor is it easy to see how an Englishman or an American could be injured morally by this book, for the " *milieu* " is entirely different from his own. I should rather say, notwithstanding the style and many delightful passages, that the work is not so much immoral as " nasty."

The chief argument in favor of such a story as " Bel-Ami " (taken as a whole) is the scientific.

That, of course, makes for the justification of its morality. Is it not well to have presented pictures of society of all sorts as it is? This is the contention of the naturalistic writers. In a former chapter we considered the danger to art contained in their theory. In the moral question, however, the " naturalists " hold a strong position. If their novels were only read by the reflective and earnest, they could not be opposed successfully on the moral side; but such is not the case, while the special argument arising from the peculiar susceptibility of the erotic appetite to be fed by description still remains in force.

Mr. W. L. Alden, in a magazine article,* maintains that violations of the seventh commandment must necessarily enter largely into fictitious literature because of the subjective, analytical character of the modern novel. Stories for the most part deal with social life. Into this love enters to a prevailing degree, and all the passion and the impulses connected with it must become a theme for description. It is in departures from the normal, the ordinary, that the incidents are found which are requisite for interest. M. Daudet also remarks: " Adultery with all its dangers, its emotions, never fails to attract." † There is truth in these observations. But if some characters in a story commit adultery, it is pleasant to find

---

* The *Galaxy*.　　　† " Thirty Years of Paris."

some who do not and who would not if they had a chance.   There are such people in the world, but we do not discover them in " Bel-Ami," unless, perhaps, the very old people.   Hence the justice of Mr. Henry James's remark about this particular story : " The world represented is too special, too little inevitable, too much to take or leave as we like—a world in which every man is a cad and every woman a harlot."*   It seems a pity that a man of so great literary genius should introduce his readers to a company of such tiresome and sickening characters.   If there had been one person of a different type, so as to exhibit a contrast, the effect would have been incalculably better—like that produced by Vera and Corrèze, in Ouida's " Moths," for example.

But we must be reasonable about these matters. It is to be regretted that there exists in America a provincial prudery for which the birch-rod is the only appropriate medicine.   With people of this ilk, a single expression is quite sufficient to kill a novel in their estimation ; much more a situation which develops illicit associations.   They are represented by the ancient fossil to whom I made reference a few pages back, who objected to an account of young men getting drunk at Delmonico's. They are also to be found, it seems, among the governors of young ladies' seminaries, like those of

---

* " Partial Portraits."

Wellesley College, who condemned Dr. Edward Eggleston's "Roxy" as not suitable for their library. Now, people who would reject "Roxy" would have spat upon and buffeted Jesus of Nazareth; while the thieves who were crucified with him would be too good company for them. So we often observe both men and women shuddering with horror at the discussion of current French novels, or at finding these stories on the table of a friend. It is the same sort we discover draping nude statues, as at the Detroit Museum. And again in journalism we notice them (I think with more affectation than sincerity), condemning, for instance, a book like the Marquise Lanza's "Modern Marriage," because, though the tendency of the work is moral and its execution highly artistic, it contains an account of a married woman visiting the apartments of her lover. Then they abuse the author because she dedicated such a tale to her young sons! So, it will be remembered, Charlotte Brontë's "Jane Eyre" was pronounced too immoral to be ranked as decent literature; George Eliot's "Adam Bede" was characterized as the "vile outpourings of a lewd woman's mind"; and Mrs. Browning's "Aurora Leigh" was described as the "hysterical indecencies of an erotic mind." People possessed with sentiments so extreme cannot be argued with. They can be taught nothing. They can sometimes be whipped into silence, but that is all. Those, however, who, though better

than they, are yet inclined to be more respectful
to their ideas and are forming their own, would do
well to study the many noble works which, either
by criticism of individuals or by general discussion, profoundly deal with art in general and
literary art in particular. Then the eye will
see more clearly and the mind apprehend more
readily. The proper universality of art will be
understood, and the remarks of Mr. Henry James
to the young novelist will be appreciated as embracing the best and profoundest philosophy:
"All life belongs to you, and don't listen either
to those who would shut you up in corners of it
and tell you that it is only here and there that art
inhabits, or to those who would persuade you that
this heavenly messenger wings her way outside of
life altogether, breathing a superfine air, and turning away her head from the truth of things. There
is no impression of life, no manner of seeing it and
feeling it, to which the plan of the novelist may
not offer a place." * Then, on the special question
of morality and immorality, there is an excellent
thought contained in the following language of R.
Buchanan : † "An immoral subject, treated insin-
cerely, leaves an immoral effect on those natures
weak enough to be influenced by it at all. The
same subject, treated with the power of genius
and the delicacy of art, delights and exalts us. In

---

* "The Art of Fiction."   † *Fortnightly Review*, vol. vi., 1866.

the pure white light of the author's sincerity and the delicate tints of literary loveliness, the immoral point just shows distinctly enough to impress purely, without paining."

Assuming that proper educational precautions are taken as to immature minds, perhaps the people who are most injured by books of evil tendencies are their authors. These last we have not been particularly considering, but they ought to be considered. We have insisted all along that the author cannot be separated from his work, and that the revelation therein of the author's mind pervades the æsthetic impression made upon the beholder by the work itself. His greatness or littleness, as therein disclosed, enters largely into the estimate of his production. Readers want to see the writer's ideals and then observe how and upon what he exercises his creative powers. Into his ideal they desire to enter and to go sympathetically with the author on his way, assisting in the construction, participating in the creation. They will demand good company, not bad, and their judgment of the author's personality will be formed by the expression of thought and feeling in the language before them.

These suggestions lead up to a much broader question, into which merge all these queries respecting morality and art which we have been discussing—perhaps at too great a length. This is the general treatment of evil and good with respect

to each other in the plan of a story. The settle-
ment of this question really disposes of most of
the others, which are subordinate.

At the present writing I have before me two
newspaper articles, one entitled "The Literature
of Discontent,"* the other a criticism of M. Paul
Bourget's "Mensonges."† Two years and more
apart, the burden of their thought is the same.
They both connect, as if necessarily, erotic literature and what the first-named writer has styled
that of discontent. They both lament the prevailing pessimistic character of fiction. The first,
speaking of modern novelists, says: "There is an
increasing tendency to regard the earth as a prison-
house, and existence, in the words of Edgar Saltus,
as 'an immense, an unnecessary affliction'—until
the only wise course seems to be to find the edge
of the world and jump off into space.

.   .   .   .

"With one class of thinkers the influence of the
age produces a curious kind of paralysis; and of
this class Amiel, whose journal is one of the sad-
dest books of our time, stands as the type.

.   .   .   .

"The gloom of the materialistic writers is of
another nature; it is the revulsion of feeling that
follows a saturnalia—disgust after debauch. De-
claring that man has no to-morrow, they set to work

---

* New York *Star*, February, 1890.
† New York *Tribune*, November 27, 1887.

in their own fashion to make the most of to-day. Ignoring everything in human nature that aspires, they worship the beast in man—the 'man-swine' wallowing in the mire.

"Everywhere they show us 'sense-quenching soul.' They turn their eyes from the rainbow vision written across the skies to the filth of the pig-sty, and say: 'This is all of life.' The struggle for existence, as represented by them, is not like the battling of wild beasts, which has at least the savage nobility of strength, but rather like the horrible writhing and rending of the lowest forms of life, seen through the microscope. In common consistency, these wise men should be happy; yet their to-day, for all its clatter, is not even merry. Pleasures and dissipations and all of the ingenuities of vice outworn, at last we find them sitting, grim and gray, amid the débris of the feast, muttering complaints against the emptiness and hollowness of life."

The other writer observes: "The modern psychologic novelist believes in nothing but the persistence of evil. There is neither faith nor virtue in man or woman for him. Everything is for the worst in the worst possible world. The heavens are brass and the earth iron. What the old profligate, Jean de Meung, wrote about women in the fourteenth century is reproduced, only in a more polished form, at the close of the nineteenth. It is the *credo* of the French romancer, whether psychologist or realist. And what is the goal to which all this tends? There is no thought of a higher life. There is no feeling after spiritual development. The conception of severe suffering experienced on the fleshly plane never suggests the ascent of the soul to a loftier eminence and a purer atmosphere."

He then expresses the following conclusions: "Surely this is a literature alike depressing and demoralizing, a literature in which false psychology masquerades in company with false morals and false art; a literature unfaithful to the foundation principles of art, in fact, since it turns its back at once upon the beautiful and the true."

While there is danger of applying the above remarks to a greater number of books and authors than the facts warrant, there is no doubt that they properly characterize the color and tone of many modern novels. But though the erotic and the pessimistic are frequently associated, as in M. Bourget's works, the latter is found without the former, as in Turgénieff's stories, and the former without the latter, as in "Mademoiselle de Maupin." Any philosophy which lays great stress on seizing the enjoyments of to-day implies want of faith in the to-morrow. Moreover, the excess apt to follow when one acts on these ideas produces an exhaustion which issues in hopelessness and despair. But such despair may come from other reasons. The pessimism of the Russian writers arises, doubtless, from the political and social conditions of their country. Balzac certainly does not exhibit a very hopeful or exhilarating prospect of human life, unless, perhaps, when he gets to "Louis Lambert" and "Seraphita;" but he shows the workings of all sorts of passions besides the erotic. M. de Maupassant, on the other hand, deals almost wholly, one might even say, with sexual relations, and he is also a pessimist. The erotic mania is, however, not the sole cause of pessimism, which may develop from the indulgence of strong promptings of appetite, from the sense of one's inability to realize ideals, from failure of effort, and from oppressive conditions of life of any sort.

It is clear enough that oftentimes the feeling of the omnipresence and omnipotence of evil possesses the human mind, and with many people it is always the case that "the heavens are brass and the earth iron." But how should the artist look upon these conditions, and what are his relations to them? For one, I am strongly of the opinion expressed in the criticism of "Mensonges" just quoted, that the pessimistic plan in a novel is "unfaithful to the foundation principles of art, . . . since it turns its back at once upon the beautiful and the true." The field of art is not restricted to what is, but the whole region of the possible is opened up to the artist. It is for him to create, and those who are to look upon his work will always expect his creation to be something which they can appreciate and enjoy as satisfying their own ideals of improvement on present conditions. The great majority of readers of a novel, those who form public opinion at least, are bound to say: Since life is full of care and trouble, and since there is a possible world better than what we experience, into which you, the artist, if you be an artist, may enter; introduce us within, and make for us a society that shall be a refreshing contrast to that of which we . are a part. Give us examples of the best in human nature, not the worst. If our atmosphere be murky with evil, lift us up into a clearer air, which shall invigorate us as we breathe it, making .us more buoyant and hopeful. What use have we for books which merely recall the sordid and tiresome struggle into which we are forced in our business or social activity? We want to be taken away from that to behold something charming, delightful, and exhilarating !

These sentiments are not only natural, but they are much more universal than novel-writers seem to suppose. Moreover, they express a correct idea of art. A story which " leaves a bad taste in the mouth," a tale which wearies and depresses, is deficient on the artistic side. It is a work in which an essential principle of art is ignored or violated—namely, the minimizing of the disagreeable. If, however, that principle be observed, it

will atone for a great many artistic defects. E. P. Roe saw this, and that is one secret of the success of his writings. He says, in a review article: *
"The elements of light and hopefulness are essential to a living novel. There may be plenty of tragedy, but this should be shadow in the picture ; and no true, pleasing picture can be painted in black or in lurid reds alone. A story cannot hold a large place among the living which leaves an unredeemed impression of horror or even of despondency." "If it leaves them (the readers) more relaxed morally, more disheartened and hopeless, no art can save the story in their estimation." To such testimony let me add a word from Professor Boyesen: † "Art can engage in no better pursuit than to stimulate noble and healthful thought on all matters of human concern, and thereby clear the prejudiced mind and raise the average of human happiness."

The novel must revivify. It must quicken like the sunlight. It must rejoice one like the cool, delicious breeze. It must inspire like the face and conversation of an admirable friend. It must lead us out from aridity into green pastures. If it makes us sorrowful, it must also give us solace to relieve our suffering. If it exhibit terrible things, it must at the same time make our souls strong to bear them, and fill us with the courage to resist

* The *Forum*.   † *Ibid.*

evil.   Unless it accomplish these results, it is not a work of the best art.   "Art has for its highest function to satisfy our emotions by an ideal presentment of life." *

But once more comes forward our scientific advocate, who reminds us of the advantages of a knowledge of evil as well as of good.   We must treat him with respect, for he has a considerable power of argument on his side.   Yet it seems to me he cannot overcome our contention that science in the novel is not good enough science, and tends to spoil art.   It is, however, true that we are not able to obtain accurate pictures of individual character and social conditions anywhere save in fiction. M. Zola's works have a scientific value.   It is not to be regretted that they exist.   The difficulty is, being successful, they establish a fashion in literature which is pernicious.   Every tyro in fiction-writing thinks he must imitate them.   Now, if all story-writers were Zolas, the art of fiction would straightway perish.   Everything runs to extremes ; to regulate and balance is hard.   If once we get into the way of thinking that the study of social facts means the unpleasant ones, that analysis of character means only hunting for the sensual, the ignoble, and the pessimistic, we shall be losing the best things of life, which lie all around us if we would only observe and use them.   We shall, in-

---

* James Sully, The *Forum*, August, 1890.

deed, be turning our backs on the beautiful and the true.

It is greatly to be feared that many of those who make use of scientific claims as justification for "naturalistic" writing are not sincere. They are glad of an excuse to dwell on subjects they like to contemplate, but which would be eschewed by people of better taste. If this be slanderous, it may at least be said that they have very superficial ideas of what science is. They do not pursue the true scientific methods with any thoroughness. This was remarked in Chapter VI., and this I must again and here impress. They do not disclose the light side, which exists just as truly as the dark. They omit redeeming features; they do not recognize the healthy forces, but only the disease-producing. In painting a picture of social life they use only the lurid reds and the dark colors. If we may not bring a like charge against all the "naturalists," such is the prevailing tendency of many of them. They do not give a scientific account, because they do not show evil and good in society, or the individual, in their true relations. They never find the soul of goodness in things evil. They look upon the aspect of dissolution rather than on that of evolution. Their work is scientifically imperfect. The nature of their task is such that they must use their selective faculties. They must form a plan and adapt materials to it. When this is done under a false ideal, which ignores the governing principles of art, there results a composition which is neither one thing nor the other; satisfying neither the scientific nor the æsthetic sentiments.

The only true theory of the novel is that which places the artistic foremost. But the truly great artist is he who has the noblest and best ideals. These can alone exist in a mind broad and profound; in a character loving truth, having a fulness of moral sentiment, possessing a tender sympathy with human wants, and an unquenchable faith in the eternal and immortal—not indeed as defined by formulas and creeds, but as an ever-living, inexhaustible source of creative power, in the exercise of which man by labor and aspiration may participate. Then over and beyond the dismal prospect of the world's woe rises always the vision of the heavens we would construct, and which, when we lift up our eyes to their glories, draw us unto them. It is in the presence of a soul forever seeing such visions that we behold the great artist. When in the Medicean chapel we gaze upon the four "ineffable figures" that symbolize together the weariness and the hope of humanity, the sleep and the resurrection, the dawn following the darkness, we stand in awe, thinking not of the incompleteness of the work. Realism it is, but it is "transfigured realism"; and we go forth admiring and fearing, knowing that we have been face to face with the work of sublime creative genius, understanding that it is such because it takes hold of the imperishable, links our souls to the divine, and speaks to us with that voice of power whose utterances, as Sophocles says, "are not of to-day, nor of yesterday, and no man can tell when they came." *

He who would become a novelist, therefore, should understand that when he has made himself great enough and good enough, he will write good novels. He will have a message to communicate to his fellows, and that may be through a very simple plan and the use of very commonplace materials. But in his hands they will, perchance, not be commonplace. He will not be troubled over questions of realism or romanticism, nor need he concern himself much about morality or immorality; he will be moral despite himself. It will matter little whether or not he introduce murderers or mistresses. He can create Hydes as well as Jekylls. He will have the freedom of a clear head and a sound heart. Says Arréat: "*Une œuvre vraiment belle, en somme, est une œuvre* SAINE." † But if he would preserve his liberty, he must not forget that his readers expect to be cheered, inspired, and improved by his books. As Mr. Sully says: He must give the predominant place to "what is lovely and of good report; the aspects of character and experience

---

* "Antigone": 456.
† "In fine, a work truly beautiful is a healthy work."

which gladden the imagination, and by gladdening it, inspire hope and faith." *

We may assert, in the language of M. David-Sauvageot,† that pessimism is "*un désordre artistique dont la cause est assez souvent un désordre moral ;*" and we may be quite sure that the poet's words express true philosophy:

> " That Beauty, Good, and Knowledge are three sisters,
>   That dote upon each other, friends to man,
>   Living together under the same roof,
>   And never can be sundered without tears." ‡

---

* The *Forum*, August, 1890.

† " Le Realisme et le Naturalisme," etc.—" An artistic disorder of which the cause is too frequently a moral disease."

‡ Tennyson.

CHAPTER XIV.

THE CONSTRUCTION OF A WORK OF FICTION.

It would be presumptuous for me to lay down law to the masters of fiction-writing with regard to the practice of their own art. Many of these writers have given the world theories as well as examples of how, in their judgment, novels should be constructed. Since I have never entered into this field of literary composition, it would no doubt be just, in case I should attempt to give directions, if some experienced writer should rebuke me as Napoleon did the too eager youth at Jena : " Wait till you have commanded in twenty pitched battles before you presume to offer advice." It probably would not be necessary for me to write twenty novels in order to entitle me to express an opinion as to what sort of construction is likely to please a reader. If reading novels, however, will compensate for failing to write them, in affording knowledge which suffices for the purposes of critical suggestion, I can probably qualify. But I shall certainly be as modest as my nature will allow in treating the special topic at the head of this chapter. I shall only venture to make a few desultory remarks which occur to me as a proper supplement to what has been already advanced in the preceding pages.

In the first place, it seems quite evident that the short-story is likely to become increasingly more favored by the reading public. A number of causes combine to produce this result. People in active business who like to read have not the time for anything which requires a long sitting. If the story reaches beyond the limit, there is no telling when the next opportunity will occur; the thread of connection is broken, the interest is abated, and a feeling of dissatisfaction ensues, making the reader reluctant to take up a book which will need for its perusal more than one session. These difficulties present themselves in their extreme form in the serial, that abomination of magazine literature. Since such productions appear, they are doubtless acceptable to some, or the editors would stop them. The fact, however, that a serial story can be endured makes us wonder what sort of people there are in this world of ours, and gives one a very profound impression of the infinite and amazing variety exemplified in the development of the human mind. The English three-volume custom is another outrage on readers. Still, such novels are read mostly by those who have been educated down to them; and men can be trained to endure anything, and say they like it, too.

Not only is there lack of time to read, but there is less time to read *novels*, than formerly. By this I mean that the multiplication of books, periodicals, and newspapers has produced a great increase of works in all departments of literature. The opportunities exist for a wider range in the reader's choice as to what he shall spend his time upon. News, travels, essays, history, science, art— all are afforded to him in great abundance. And not only is the quantity of works in these departments increasing, but the quality is improving. A higher cultivation demands that all such books be made interesting. The artistic form is necessitated more and more in all literary productions. Hence we have science popularized, essays made entertaining, and even philosophy made readable—but on this last topic I prefer not to dwell! The novelist of the present day has, then, no monopoly in the business of furnishing interesting reading. If, in the delusion that he has, he recklessly expands his works, as members of his guild did not hesitate to do fifty years ago, he will soon come to be regarded as a nuisance and find none so poor as to do him reverence. These millennial days of public opinion, it must be confessed, have not yet arrived, but the early dawn is visible at any rate, and story-writers should be wise in time. Even if the signs are wrong, and it is only the false dawn, the real one is sure to follow.

From the same considerations, it further appears that a diminished length of the story is not all that is required. Mr. Brander Matthews * urges that there is a distinct difference between the short-story and the story which is merely short. The chief requisites of the former " are compression, originality, ingenuity, and now and again a touch of fantasy." This is to say, after all, that people, in their gratitude to an author for making his story short, will not think it good solely because it is not so long as it might have been. It must, in addition, be striking and interesting. It must be well made. Mr. Matthews admits that the " short-story and the sketch, the novel and the romance melt and merge one into the other, and no man may mete the boundaries of each, though their extremes lie far apart." We may not go so far as to say that the short-story, as Mr. Matthews defines it, will eventually supersede the other varieties of fiction composition, but we may assert that the reading public will more and more require stories which are short, and among these the short-story will always find favor. If, however, novels proper be written, we cannot dispense with that same " compression, originality, and ingenuity" which are necessary for the short-story.

In this view, two modern writers may, perhaps, be selected as models for construction, so far as

---

* " Philosophy of the Short-Story."

form and method are concerned, leaving out subject-matter and idiosyncrasies of style. These
are Turgénieff and M. Guy de Maupassant. In
neither of these is there anything superfluous. (I
do not speak of some of the earlier tales of the
last-named, every word of which, including the
title, is superfluous.) But the unity of the composition in most of their stories is clear and satisfying. The art of compression they have learned
perfectly. He would be of a strange mental
nature who would be bored by either. Their
tales present each a picture, with well-coördinated
and organically related parts. Hence, their stories
hold the attention of the reader concentrated,
and make the impression upon him of a distinct
and finished work of art. Their excellence in this
respect is very plainly seen by a contrast with
Tolstoï, for example, in some of his productions.
" Anna Karénina " is a good one to take. . This is
really two novels in one. It is a history of the
Karénin family and of the Levin family. To
give my own experience with the book : I discovered this fact early in the reading, and found that,
by omitting the chapters pertaining chiefly to the
Levins, I could follow the thread of the Karénin
fortunes to the end without any hiatus being observable. This I did, and then returned to read
the Levin story. Of course the contrasts between
the characters and the lives of the two families
are instructive, but the incidents are not so inter-

woven as to form a single, unified work of art. In the progress of reading, one frequently feels like saying, as Rudyard Kipling does, when in his tales he strikes upon some incident foreign to his immediate purpose of narration, " But that is another story ; " and wishing that the author had postponed telling it till another time. Precisely the same fault is found in Mr. Henry James's " Tragic Music," and it often occurs in literature.

The lack of simplicity in the plan of a novel is a great drawback to its perfection. In former times it seems as if complexity of incident and a succession of startling events were deemed absolutely essential to interest. This was a part of the philosophy of the romanticists. It was not so long ago that George Sand was in vogue. Admirable as she is in many respects, after acquaintance with such writers as Turgénieff and M. de Maupassant, what ill-jointed, roughly constructed, half-done productions her stories appear to be ! A tale of Turgénieff is a perfect marble statue ; a story of George Sand, by comparison, a manikin of *papier maché !* The readers of " Consuelo " will remember how the author racked their nerves, until they were fairly in agony, with an interminable series of adventures, enough for a dozen novels. Then, not content with this, she writes a sequel to the tale—the " Countess of Rudolstadt." From such novel-writers, good Lord, deliver us !

The principle of unity and simplicity forbids diffuseness in description of scenes, of places, or of persons. Ouida's " In Maremma " Mr. Edgar Fawcett calls "a tale of matchless grace and sweetness." So it is ; but it would have been infinitely better if the author had spared us the endless and tiresome repetition of description of "the sultry heavens," "the torpid sea," "the gray sky parched with mists of intense heat," "the fever fog," and "the glaring sands." Let the reader study Charles Reade's " Cloister and the Hearth," and note the difference. The fault of long narrative accounts of characters instead of making them reveal themselves by speech and action is not now very common among writers of reputation; but when it occurs it is a serious blemish, because, if the work were well done, it is quite unnecessary ànd is at best a clumsy method of portrayal.

Again, the artistic effect is much impaired by the introduction of homilies, disquisitions, arguments, and speculations, not required by the plan of work. Bulwer's " Strange Story " has many pages of this sort of digression which is exceedingly injurious to the force of the tale. He even argues in foot-notes for the probability of what he states in the text. What a refreshing contrast to this is Mr. Stevenson's " Jekyll and Hyde," a most admirably constructed story, in which artistic requirements are perfectly fulfilled and the readers feel no lack of information or explanation as to the subject-matter. A still worse kind of perversion of the novel occurs where the moralizing and philosophizing are the main thing, the story being subordinated thereto. Balzac's " Seraphita " is an example in point, though it must be confessed he has clothed his Swedenborgian philosophy with beautiful drapery. Yet the long expositions of Swedenborg, and commentaries on his ideas, are tiresome and quite unnecessary. So in Tolstoï's " Kreutzer Sonata," one reads with the prevailing consciousness that the murder of the wife is only a device to hold the attention while the author throws at you his nauseating moralizing. Even M. de Maupassant has done this same thing, once at least, in " L'Inutile Beauté," where he gives one chapter of digression, for the sake of philosophizing on sexual relations ; but he is short and concise, and under such conditions a writer may sometimes be forgiven for the fault of which I have been speaking. In fine, we must agree with Señor Valéra, when he exclaims in the preface of " Pepita Ximenez " : " I think it in very bad taste, always impertinent, and often pedantic, to attempt to prove theses by writing stories. For such a purpose dissertations or books purely and severely didactic should be written."

In the light of the foregoing considerations we may enunciate as the first rule of fiction construction :

1. *Form a plan of something distinct and definite to be done.*

To this I should add two more rules, namely:

2. *Do that and nothing else in each case.*

3. *Do it well.*

If these rules be very general, they are not, I trust, meaningless from vagueness. The first and second have perhaps been sufficiently illustrated; but if the reader cares to turn back to Chapter VI., at page 79, he will find in a quotation from an article by Mr. Stevenson, the second rule emphasized. To what is said there may be added another passage from the same article: "Our art is occupied, and bound to be occupied, not so much in making stories true as in making them typical; not so much in capturing the lineaments of each fact, as in marshalling all of them toward a common end."

Apropos of forming the plan, just a word more may be said upon the choice of subjects, which is to call attention again to the greater chances of success afforded to him who is a close observer of the signs of the times, and quick to understand and sympathize with current intellectual and social movements. He must comprehend the prevailing "world-mood" of his own constituency. This changes frequently, and what will be received to-day may not be to-morrow. Those who depict contemporary life, if they are thorough students, are most certain to produce stories of a high quality of interest at the time they are published, which, in the case of a novel, is necessary to its permanent recognition. "The first object of a novelist," remarks Bulwer, "is to interest the reader; the next object is the quality of the interest. Interest in his story is essential, or he will not be read; but if the quality of the interest is not high, he will not be read a second time. And if he be not read a second time by his own contemporaries, the chance is he will not be read once by posterity."

The fact that they have accurately grasped the underlying motives of contemporaneous life, and thus been able to picture it vividly, has insured success to writers widely different in mental constitution, in tastes, and spheres of observation. People would not be apt to compare Disraeli, Turgénieff, and Dr. Edward Eggleston; yet each, within his own field of observation, has successfully done the same kind of work. The first surveyed the world of English aristocratic society; the second, the Russian middle class and peasantry; the third, the life of American communities in the West in their formative stages. The works of all three have attained a permanent place in literature. Of Disraeli it has been justly said that his novels "reflect the world he lived in and show the characteristics of its society as no novels have done since then."* The same thing is per-

---

* Ouida: *North American Review.*

fectly true of the others. Rénan's beautiful funeral tribute to Turgénieff expresses the completeness of that author's understanding of his own people, wherein he refers to Turgénieff as "the incarnation of a whole race." And what Mr. Henry James said of the great Russian is applicable to the others as well, and to all those writers who have written successful stories portraying phases of contemporary life. "This is the strength of his representations of character: .they are so strangely, fascinatingly particular, and yet they are so recognizably general."* To this we may add a word from the Marquise Lanza's "Plea for the National Element in American Fiction":† "It is, moreover, a significant truth, that every really great writer of fiction the world has ever seen, not only has expressed a wide and tender sympathy with all humanity, so to speak, but has persistently emulated in his work the national character he is fitted to comprehend."

Now, as to the third rule of construction, *Do it well*, I have no more to say than I have already said. I am afraid of the criticism of the masters, who would see my weakness, and find out too thoroughly that, though I may preach, I cannot practise. Hence my precepts would be despised. I would rather refer the reader to such passages of Ruskin as I quoted at the beginning of Chapter VI.;

---

* " Partial Portraits " : Ivan Turgénieff.

† *Cosmopolitan Magazine,* August, 1890.

to the hints given in our discussion of Realism and Idealism throughout that chapter ; to Mr. Walter Besant's "Art of Fiction," and Mr. Henry James's comments thereon ; to Mr. Stevenson's article ; to Valéra and Valdez ; and, above all, to the preface of "Pierre et Jean," by M. de Maupassant. I ought not to quote this last further than I have, but I know of nothing more admirable. Fortunate would it be for our novelists if they all had had a Flaubert to instruct, to restrain, to guide. What wisdom in his precepts ! " The smallest object contains something unknown. Find it." " Whatever be the thing one wishes to say, there is only one noun to express it, only one verb to give it life, only one adjective to qualify it. Search, then, till that noun, that verb, that adjective, are discovered. Never be content with 'very nearly'; never have recourse to tricks, however happy, or to buffooneries of language, to avoid a difficulty. We can interpret and describe the most subtile things if we bear in mind the verse of Boileau :

" ' D'un mot mis en sa place enseigna le pouvoir.' " *

In the same essay there is one other injunction that I will repeat in closing this chapter : " Keep on working. . . . Talent is long patience."

---

* Preface of " Pierre et Jean."

CHAPTER XV.

THE CRITICISM OF A WORK OF FICTION.

IF a personal reference may be pardoned—in 1884 the present writer published a systematic work on Psychology, in two large octavo volumes. This book was noticed extensively in England, also in America and on the Continent of Europe. There were reviews whose general tone was favorable, and also some unfavorable. In most of the notices, the grounds of favor or disfavor were stated. Comparison shows that every feature of the work condemned by any one was praised by some one else; while many things spoken of as special excellences were mentioned by others as conspicuous faults. One critic thought the author was weak in analysis, but strong in synthesis; another reviewer said exactly the reverse. One was "struck by the thoroughly popular nature of the exposition;" another regards it as very "abstruse and tedious." Still another speaks of the writer as "too modest;" but a more discerning critic sees through him, and speaks of him as illustrating "the vanity of modesty." One reviewer considers that he "shows hardly a sign of acquaintance with modern Continental psychology;" another, that "his perfect acquaintance with its * literature is evident on every page." The illustration of pleasures and pains by literary quotations is commended in one notice, sneered at in a second, and reprobated as unphilosophical in a third. Finally one reviewer observes that in the polemical discussion of "intuitions" and "necessary truths" the author appears at his best; while a fellow critic declares they have no place in the book, and are of no value.

What can an author think of himself and his book after reading and comparing such criticisms? It must be remembered that, in the case of the work in question, the notices were supposably written by specialists, familiar with the subject, and of about the same grade of competency. If, under such circumstances, such a contrariety of opinion was developed, what can we expect from the criticism of works of fiction, which people may and generally do value according to their own tastes and fancies of style, subject-matter, morality, or anything else, without study or reflection?

The truth of the matter is, the greater part of published criticisms of novels and stories is meaningless. It signifies nothing at all, though often full of sound and fury. It abounds in adjective characterization, which indicates the emotions of

* Psychological.

the writer but conveys no ideas. If a man eat good melon, but, being unhealthy, is distressed thereby, and he groans, must the melon at once be denounced? Said Lichtenberg, the German scientist: "If a head and a book come into collision and a hollow sound ensues, must this necessarily be attributed to the book?" If I read in a notice merely that a certain tale is "very excellent" or "very poor," I get no basis for any intelligent judgment. If there be a flux of disparaging adjectives, I may, indeed, be led unthinkingly to sympathize with the writer's feeling, as I would with the impassioned harangues of the political assembly, or the exhortations of a Moody-and-Sankey meeting. In this I may do great injustice to the writer. My prejudice harms him and prevents me from gaining knowledge, thereby injuring me as well. But this style of criticism is much more common than any better one. It substitutes inflammatory words for thought. Its effect is that of the tom-tom or the war-dance of the savage, with its leaping and shouting. Have novels become such a nuisance that their authors must be rushed at with the tomahawk and scalping-knife? Possibly it may come to this, if story-writers do not heed the excellent counsel contained in this essay! But, at all events, it is divine to forgive, and much nobler to let mercy temper justice.

Two very important articles on this subject have recently been published, in consequence of whose appearance the present chapter will be much shorter than otherwise it would have been. One of these is by Archdeacon Farrar in the *Forum ;* * the other by Mr. Howells in *Harper's Magazine.*† To these might be added a valuable paper by Mr. Fawcett entitled " Should Critics be Gentlemen?"‡ Mr. Howells thinks that "nearly all current criticism as practised among English and Americans is falsely principled and is conditioned in evil. It is falsely principled because it is unprincipled, or without principles; and it is conditioned in evil because it is almost wholly anonymous." Mr. Howells makes a strong argument against anonymous criticism, and one which seems to me unanswerable. He speaks in behalf of the reading public, not the author ; and from this point of view the gain to be derived from the opposite course would be very great, for many reasons which he gives and which I will not repeat. Mr. Howells's own comments on books in the Editor's Study, the literary notes of Mr. Laurence Hutton, and the review articles in the New York *Sun* signed " M. W. H."—whom everybody knows §—are certainly much more valuable than the general run of anonymous criticism. This value does not depend upon the reputation of the writer so much as it does on the fact that the signing of a name is a guarantee of all the thoroughness and honesty that self-

---

* May, 1890.   † August, 1890, Editor's Study.
‡ " Agnosticism and Other Essays."   § M. W. Hasseltine.

respect will induce in a critic. We can be somewhat sure of his fidelity to himself, at any rate; and knowing him we can understand his biases and prejudices sufficiently to correct in our own minds his erroneous judgments. There are frequently published, of course, good reviews whose authorship is not made known ; but in the best of the newspapers following that system there are so many notices so outrageously unfair, so biassed and jaundiced, so destitute even of comprehension of the work criticised, as to make one lose all confidence in the literary department itself, and to quite justify anything that is said in the three articles above mentioned on the iniquity of journalistic criticism.

It seems a pity Mr. Fawcett's suggestion cannot be adopted, to the effect that publishers should cease sending copies of books for review to newspapers generally. Some journals publish their list of books received with the arrogant heading: " We consider mention of the receipt of a book in this column a full equivalent therefor; as regards further notice, we shall be guided wholly by the interests of our readers." The publisher would do well to send such papers a catalogue only. It is for the interest of the readers to know what books are coming out, and if the editors do not inform them it will be worse for the paper. But the fact that such announcements appear shows the need of a change in the practice, in the interest of literature. The implication is that a book is *prima facie* trash, with a presumption against it to be overcome before it is entitled to respectful consideration. We cannot believe that literature has reached this low condition, despite the great multiplication of books. It is quite true, though, that a newspaper cannot devote its whole space to book notices. Why not, then, eliminate them entirely, relegating them to journals specially devoted to literary topics? The increase in the number of such publications as " The Book-Buyer," * " Book-Chat," † " Notes on Books," ‡ and " Literary News," would make such a course far easier than formerly. One gets much more information from these issues of publishing houses than he does from the literary notices of most newspapers. If the latter will not have signed criticisms, it would be a great gain if they would only publish condensed notices, stating fairly what the book is without making any attempt to characterize. Some few do precisely this, and greatly to the advantage of the reader.

To know what proper criticism is, one must study the works of writers who are truly critics. Of such, among those writing in the English language and upon works of fiction, Mr. Henry James appears to me to be the greatest living

* Chas. Scribner's Sons.
† Brentano.
‡ Longmans, Green & Co.

example. Of the French, I need only mention MM. Taine, Lemaitre, Brunetière, and Bourget. The art of criticism requires fidelity to truth and justice, an ability to weigh and compare, analytical power, a wide acquaintance with literature, a clear understanding of human nature, and a thorough knowledge of social life—the action and reaction of one mind upon another.

But while justice demands that a novel-writer be understood, that the plan of his work be comprehended, and that its execution be judged fairly, the privilege remains to the reader, more unreservedly in the case of the novel than perhaps in any other kind of literature, of saying, " I do not like it," without being obliged to justify the dislike by argument. One may choose his own company, and, if he does not enjoy one set, he is not obliged to say that he does, or to seek that coterie. One person may prefer Gaboriau and another George Eliot. From this, however, nothing could be argued as to the comparative excellence of the two authors, except, perhaps, from the characters of the readers. Yet, though our preference be decided, we must not apply it as universal law. The tendency to do so is sometimes very strong, and that is always one source of difficulty in estimating the comparative merits of novels. But I think we shall always find that, the wider the reach of their influence, the greater number of people they appeal to, the more success must they be deemed to have attained on the whole. We should, however, be careful to take into account not merely the present interest in them, but also their ability to maintain a place permanently in literature.

In closing this essay, I am constrained to repeat the words of Mr. Besant in concluding his lecture on the " Art of Fiction " : " Wherever you find good and faithful work, with truth, sympathy, and clearness of purpose, I pray you to give the author of that work the praise as to an artist—an artist like the rest—the praise that you so readily accord to the earnest student of any other art. As for the great masters of the art, . . . I for one feel irritated when the critics begin to appraise, compare, and to estimate them ; there is nothing, I think, that we can give them but admiration that is unspeakable and gratitude that is silent. This silence proves more eloquently than any words how great, how beautiful an art is that of Fiction."

THE END.

AUTHORS CITED OR QUOTED, WITH REFERENCES TO PAGES.

CRITICAL NOTICES.

A SYSTEM OF PSYCHOLOGY.

BY DANIEL GREENLEAF THOMPSON.

2 vols., 8vo, 1226 pages.

The Leeds (England) Mercury.
This is a very comprehensive and important work.

The Journal of Mental Science (England).
Mr. Thompson's work accomplishes its aim in a very successful manner.
The book may without hesitation be pronounced a good one.

The Edinburgh Scotsman.
In the seventy-five chapters of these bulky volumes a more detailed and systematic account is given of the genesis and development of states of consciousness than can be found in any other single work in the language.
Mr. Thompson is an accomplished and earnest searcher after truth.

The N. Y. Popular Science Monthly.
It is undoubtedly the most important contribution to psychological science that any American has yet produced; nor is there any foreign work with which we are acquainted that contains so exhaustive, so instructive, and well presented a digest of the subject as this.

The Academy (England).
Mr. Thompson's treatise, though named *A System of Psychology*, is in reality, in outline at least, a system of philosophy.
While following the most plainly marked track in the fields of English thought, Mr. Thompson is independent, and now and again impressively original.

The Contemporary Review (England).
Mr. Thompson is an acute and careful observer himself, and a systematic student of the results put forward by other workers.
The author has amply made good the modest claim he puts forward for himself as an independent student.—A. SETH.

1

Mind (England).

The passages that have been referred to must, of course, be taken merely as specimens of Mr. Thompson's contributions to psychology, not as a complete account of all that he has done; but they are sufficient to show that if he has not systematized the science from any new point of view, he has at least carried the analytical methods of the older psychology further in various directions.

Nature (England).

In criticising any new book, we ought to ask whether the author has made any advance on his immediate predecessors. We ought, in fact, to apply to the particular author we are criticising the test of progress to which psychology as a whole may be submitted. Mr. Thompson's book will emerge successfully from an examination such as that which is here suggested. In dealing with many special questions he goes beyond the later English psychologists, just as they themselves have gone beyond Locke.

We may conclude by saying that, although in some respects an unequal book, it is decidedly an important contribution of America to the treatment of psychology on the lines with which English readers are most familiar.

The Index (Boston, Mass.).

It is recognized as a standard work at once. (*First notice.*)

This work proves the author to be a man of large intellectual grasp, of keen critical and analytical ability, and at the same time of large constructive power and capacity for generalization, of ample acquaintance with philosophy and literature.

One need not assent to all that Mr. Thompson advances in order to appreciate his robust thought, his masterly reasoning, his clear, strong style and truly philosophic spirit. (*Second notice.*)

It is without doubt the most profound, extensive, and original work on psychology that this country has produced. (*Third notice.*)

Revue Philosophique (Paris).

We consider that Mr. Thompson has rendered a great service to psychologists in undertaking to systematize results actually attained; he has succeeded in presenting them in clear and precise form; he has in many places added useful information, and the reading of his work is eminently suggestive. It seems to us, above all, that he has the great merit of producing a work almost entirely psychological.—F. PICAVET.

THE PROBLEM OF EVIL.

BY DANIEL GREENLEAF THOMPSON.

8vo., 281 pages.

The Journal of Education (England).

Mr. Thompson has already made a name for himself as a psychologist, and he handles the questions of moral science with an acuteness which will sustain his reputation.

The N. Y. Popular Science Monthly.

A multitude of the pressing problems of our social life are suggested and discussed in this compact volume with such frankness, sincerity, ability, and good feeling that we can heartily commend it not only to the professional scholar, but to all thoughtful men and women.

The Open Court (Chicago, Ill.).

The style of our author is admirably clear, and the general tone of the discussion, covering, as it does, a wide range of practical questions which are uppermost in the thought of millions at the present day, will doubtless secure for Mr. Thompson's book a wide circle of intelligent readers.

The Guardian (England).

We admire his [*the author's*] originality and analytical power, his obvious desire to be true to facts, his almost omnivorous tastes in literature, and, above all, his extreme modesty and self-effacement. Even when we come to the end and remember that we disagree with his first principles, there remains with us a consciousness of much that is true and some things which are new, while in lucidity of exposition and fearlessness of statement Mr. Thompson reminds us more of John Stuart Mill than of any other of his chosen leaders.

Knowledge (England).

Mr. Thompson, in the very able and important work before us, investigates the nature and origin of evil, and essays to point out the most hopeful means for its elimination. . . . He discusses at length the suggested methods (social, political, and ecclesiastical) for reducing evil to a minimum, which have been and are still advanced, and shows trenchantly the fallacies which underlie them all. . . . We will not diminish the pleasure with which the reader will peruse this volume, by any more detailed analysis of its contents ; suffice it to say that Mr. Thompson has made a real and enduring contribution to ethical philosophy.

THE RELIGIOUS SENTIMENTS OF THE HUMAN MIND.

BY DANIEL GREENLEAF THOMPSON.

8vo, 184 pages.

The Popular Science Monthly (New York).

In the volume before us Mr. Thompson has entered upon a fruitful field of thought and discussion ; one, moreover, which requires great tact and delicacy in its cultivation, if the author would secure the sympathetic and respectful attention of his readers. In this respect, Mr. Thompson has been notably successful. His treatment of his topic is calm, temperate, philosophical, free from bias, appealing to reason rather than to theological or anti-theological prejudices. While his discussion of the religious problem is entirely frank, manly, and unconventional, it is also duly considerate of those conceptions which he is compelled to discredit and oppose. . . . The book, as a whole, stimulates thought and holds the attention of the reader. In connection with " A System of Psychology " and " The Problem of Evil," it justifies us in ranking its author among our ablest philosophical thinkers.

The Manchester (England) Examiner.

Readers of the more thoughtful type who are acquainted with Mr. Daniel Greenleaf Thompson's " System of Psychology," and his very suggestive treatment of " The Problem of Evil," will extend a hearty welcome to his new work. . . . Though his work cannot be compared with the recent magnificent contribution to the literature of the same great theme by Dr. James Martineau, it is full of acute, sound, and penetrating thought. Of the four sections into which the book is divided, perhaps the second . . . is the richest in interest ; but the work, from first to last, is well worthy of careful study.

Mind.

Mr. Thompson's present work is a study of the science, not of *religions* as they exist or have existed, but of *religion* as a general fact of conscious experience. His aim is rather to determine what beliefs can rationally be held about the supernatural than to describe the process by which the supernatural comes to be believed in ; though, in accordance with his traditional view of philosophic method, he makes an investigation of this preliminary to his determination of the limits of rational belief, and more generally bases his religious philosophy on his previous work in psychology and ethics.

SOCIAL PROGRESS.

BY DANIEL GREENLEAF THOMPSON.

8vo, 182 pages.

New York Times.

There is a matter of exceeding interest to be found in this volume, which is a cool and dispassionate analysis of human actions.

Boston Transcript.

The book is full of meat for thoughtful readers. . . . We commend it to the reading of every man who wishes to see the way clearer to political and social reform in our own country.

Edinburgh Scotsman.

An admirable, clear, and logical exposition of those principles which are now generally recognized as the essential conditions of national and individual well being.

Science.

The author's style is clear and flowing, so that the book is easy and agreeable to read ; and there is much in it that thinkers of all schools will agree with.

The Epoch.

Mr. Thompson shows great analytical power, clearness of statement, moderateness of view, and frequently originality. This book might well be read by every American citizen, for even old thoughts are put in a forcible, and often original, way.

The Christian Union.

The best part of Mr. Thompson's book is that in which he discusses ʻoral and religious ideas. He urges the duty of intellectual hospitality, ʻd himself recognizes it in his treatment of Christian ideas which he does ʻt accept. He urges upon Christian people a willingness to let those who ʻfer with them in faith unite with them in good works, reminding them the Scripture teaching that those who " do the will " shall " know the ʻtrine.

American Hebrew.

ʻn important and valuable contribution to political science. He evinces asterly logical equipment. His eduction of the principles of liberty equality is certainly to be classed with the very best specimens of close ʻning upon abstract subjects. Mr. Thompson has contributed a worthy ʻion to the literature of philosophical thought ; his speculative genius ʻfound and broad enough to give him high rank not only among the ʻlect thinkers in America, but among the acutest metaphysicians of ʻe.

www.ingramcontent.com/pod-product-compliance
Lightning Source LLC
Chambersburg PA
CBHW020115030726
47498CB00006B/2109